An Accidental Diplomat

Published 2021 in Great Britain by PostcardBooks
Part of EnvelopeBooks: envelopebooks.co.uk
A New Premises venture

PostcardBooks
12 Wellfield Avenue
London N10 2EA

Cover design: Stephen Games | Booklaunch

Photograph page 49 courtesy of Associated Newspapers Ltd

A CIP catalogue record for this title is available from the British Library.

PostcardBook 3
ISBN 9781915023018

Designed and edited by Booklaunch for PostcardBooks
www.postcardbooks.org

An Accidental Diplomat

Nigel Thorpe

POSTCARD BOOKS

About the author

Nigel Thorpe (born 1945) grew up in South London before moving, aged eleven, to East Grinstead, where he attended the grammar school. After gaining a first-class honours degree in History from University College, Cardiff, he joined HM Diplomatic Service. As well as positions in London, especially as head of Central European Department (1992–96), he served in Poland (twice), Bangladesh, Canada and Zimbabwe, finishing his career as ambassador to Hungary (1998–2003). He then worked for Vodafone before immersing himself in voluntary work in London. He has been married twice and treasures his children and grandson.

Contents

Introduction

It is April 1998. I am in Budapest, the capital city of Hungary, by now a democracy free of the Soviet Union and Communism. Moreover, I am sitting with the President of Hungary, having just presented my credentials as British Ambassador to his country. I am excited and a little overwhelmed. Everyone is calling me 'Excellency' which I am not (yet) used to. I have a chauffeur outside, in a British racing green Jaguar which flies the Union Jack, waiting to drive me to the Tomb of the Unknown Warrior where I shall lay a wreath. Is this really me? How on earth did all this happen? I was just an ordinary boy from South London with no expectations of anything as a child or even a young adult. What happened? It is a curious tale: of bad judgements, good timing and luck. Here is my story.

Childhood

I grew up in the shadow of the Second World War. I was born in October 1945, the year the war ended in Europe (in May) and then in the East, in July. I lived with my parents and sister in south London, at first in Shirley (technically in Surrey then), and then in Thornton Heath, which was much more urban. There were bomb sites everywhere, great gaps between houses where rubble had been cleared, and here and there odd house walls standing alone. The regular trip with my mother to collect the family ration book seemed normal.

London was drab, very grey and downbeat. There were few cars on the road and people were poorly dressed. I suppose there was not much in the shops either but I did not notice that. I had never seen a different world and so did not question the one I found myself in. I did ask about what I saw around me. In answer to my questions my parents explained the war as they understood it and had experienced it. I learnt about the Blitz, about the V bombs (doodlebugs and the V2 rocket), I played with ammunition clips discarded from aircraft that had fought over our house (they made an excellent mortar for my toy soldiers). I learnt especially about the Dunkirk evacuation and of course about Winston Churchill who had saved not just Britain but Europe from the Nazis.

When I was old enough I read some of the many books being written about the war, especially those of prisoners of war who escaped from German or Japanese captivity. My parents had an ex-army trenching tool and I used this to play Prisoners of War in our garden and dig the beginnings of tunnels through which to escape. Occasionally I was taken to the cinema to see a film, often about the war too—*The Dambusters* was a great favourite. I can still hum the theme music, written by Eric Coates. We also learnt about the war at school, mainly by anecdote from our teachers, some of whom had taken part in it. One blamed his baldness on having to wear a helmet for so long.

I realise now that for my parents, the war defined them. It is odd to say but the war was the most exciting time of their lives. They talked about it till they died. It affected the way they thought and acted, and it influenced their decisions, especially my father's. They were both young when it began—my father nineteen, my mother seventeen. My father immediately volunteered for the RAF and was taken on for training as a navigator. For reasons I never really understood he did not see active service but instead returned to his job as a technical draughtsman and worked on the naval development of the Spitfire at a company in Croydon. He was lucky in a way. He told me before he died that he believed everyone he had trained with had been killed in the bombing raids over Germany.

My mother had become a secretary on leaving school and was evacuated to Torquay in Devon with her company to avoid the bombing. She returned to London and my parents, who had, typically for the time, met at a dance in Norbury, got married in December 1942.

My sister was born in 1943 and I came along two years later. It was, I suppose, a statement of belief in the ultimate triumph of the Allies that my parents felt able to have children, a confidence that there was a future to live for. While my parents experienced the terrors of life in London under attack, many of their friends and relatives were in the armed forces, often seeing action. My mother's uncle, Sid, was a Royal Marine, and my father's younger brother a Lancaster and then Mosquito pilot. He flew thirteen missions over Germany. I learnt later how frightened he was every night before a raid and how he could never admit this to his colleagues.

One of my father's closest school friends was half Japanese. When he joined the army he was asked if he was prepared to go to the Burma campaign and fight against his father's compatriots. He said yes, knowing full well his fate were he to be captured. The father of one of my sister's close friends landed on D Day. And so on. The war was all around us. It was over but lived on, not just in what we saw but in what so many people experienced and still lived through.

It was this way throughout my childhood. Later, when my family had moved from London to East Grinstead I took my first Saturday job as a 16 year old, in the bar of the Old Felbridge Hotel. Every year the hotel hosted a reunion of the Guinea Pig Club of air crew who had been burned in their crashing aircraft. East Grinstead had been the site of pioneering plastic surgery by Sir Archibald McIndoe, and the Club was composed of former patients whose burnt bodies had been restored by his team. I served drinks at this event and talked to many of those there, all with harrowing stories and great courage. It was an education.

Against this background I grew up. London was very different in those days. We lived in an Edwardian terraced house. The only heating came from coal fires. Usually there was only one, in the living room. It was always very cold in the winter and there was often frost inside my bedroom window when I awoke in the morning. Hot water came from an electric boiler in the kitchen. If we wanted a bath my mother would carry buckets of hot water upstairs to the bathroom. This all seemed very normal. The house had what seemed to me an enormous garden where we could find hedgehogs, slow worms and, once, a lizard. I spent a lot of time playing in the garden. One day, during a fit of enthusiasm for archaeology, I found an old coin which I sent to the British Museum for identification. I still have the handwritten response from one of the curators.

The high street in Thornton Heath, a respectable lower-middle-class area (I suppose that is how it might have been termed at the time) featured a range of what you might call 'proper shops'—so, a grocer, a greengrocer, a butcher, an ironmonger and so on. I think my favourite was the fishmonger, who sold live eels. My great grandmother used to buy one and keep it in the sink overnight until she was ready to cook it. There was also a wonderful post office and stationer's, where we could buy glue and cardboard, plasticine and other materials to make things. Indeed, we were very self-sufficient and built many of the things we played with. Christmas preparations always involved sticking coloured streamers together to make paper chains.

Life was very centred on home and the family. My great grandmother—she of the live eels—lived ten minutes' walk away, my mother's mother, Nan, lived about the same distance, and my father's mother, Ma, lived next door but one. When I was very young Ma had all her other four children at home, so a visit there meant a meeting with all my father's family. Weekends always involved trips to at least one and often to all of the grandparents and great-grandparents. We walked, as we did not have a car until much later.

Grandma, my great grandmother, lived with grandpa in a rented house which had no electricity. They had coal fires and gas lighting, even in the mid 1950s when grandpa died. Grandma later moved to her daughter's, Nan's, until she too passed away. No old people's home for her. If we went to Grandma's on Saturday afternoon my father would light the gas lamps for them.

Nan, too, lived in a rented house. Her husband, my mother's father, had left her when my mother was only two and there had been a divorce, scandalous in the 1920s. Nan managed by taking in lodgers, young men from an agency of some sort, so her house was always full. We often went there during the school holidays when our mother was working and we had to be looked after.

School was Winterbourne School in Winterbourne Road, about a quarter of a mile from our house. We walked there every day, usually alone. The Infants was coeducational but the Junior School separated boys and girls. Curiously we were all in the same building but boys had the front half and the girls the back half. I not only learned to read and write here and to add up and spell and all the basics, it was where I was first tempted to read and think properly. We did all sorts of things that probably have no place on the normal syllabus but they were very enriching. We read the Greek and Roman myths and I learnt about Hercules and Mercury and Apollo, about Troy and Athens and Sparta. We read about Britain and its history and geography, even drawing county maps of England. We read poetry: one master introduced us to Keats's *Ode to Autumn*, a poem I still return to every year at that season. We also had a good dose of patriotism, thinking only good things about the British Empire and reciting Shakespeare ('This royal throne of kings, this sceptered isle') and singing Hubert Parry's 'Jerusalem' regularly. But I do not think we were any the worse for that. There was, by the way, a piano in every classroom and all the teachers could play. Singing took place every day and was a key part of our education. It was a wonderful start in a very ordinary school.

In the very cold winter of 1952–53 I became quite ill with scarlet fever. I was moved into my sister's bedroom (and she into mine—I always had the smallest bedroom in my parents' house but my sister's was not only bigger but had a fireplace so that the room could be heated in an emergency). I was there for some weeks before I recovered. I remember my father's youngest brother, who lived two doors away with my grandmother, building a big snowman in our garden, which I could see from my bedroom.

It was after this that my parents took us all away on holiday, to a caravan, for the Whitsun week. The idea was that I would benefit from this, I think. We went to West Wittering in Sussex and the caravan reeked of calor gas and it rained much of the time. But on 3 June it was the coronation of Queen Elizabeth. The owner of the site invited all the caravaners into her house where we watched the coronation on her tiny television screen. As we didn't have a television at home, I suppose I may not have seen the event at all were it not for this. And I did not know then that I would prepare the Queen's state visit to Zimbabwe in 1991 nor stay at Windsor Castle in 1999.

I was a sickly child. It was at school that one day in, I think, 1954, I became very ill. I went home and with my sister waited in the garden of our house for my mother to return from work. When she came she called the doctor. He did not know what was wrong but I was not well enough to return to school the next day and instead I just sat at home and became very sleepy and inactive.

By the weekend there was no improvement and on the Sunday the doctor came again. Again he did not know what was wrong and I think my parents must have insisted on a second opinion. Another doctor came and pronounced acute appendicitis. An ambulance was called. In those days they were white and had a metal bell on the roof which rang with the movement of the vehicle when the clapper was released. It was late at night and we roared through the streets, the bell ringing and my mother holding my hand. My father had borrowed a car from a neighbour and he drove behind the ambulance. My mother lifted me up and I can still see my father driving frantically behind us. I had emergency surgery and my appendix was removed. I spent two weeks in hospital and then returned home to recuperate. My parents, who had thought I was going to die, were much relieved (I am glad to say) and my mother gave up her job to be at home and be a full-time mother. That must have been quite a sacrifice, since we had little money, and she was in any case a bright woman who needed the stimulus of work.

My parents were very loving. Family was very important to both of them and they treasured it. My mother of course had been deprived of her father, whom she never knew. My father was the eldest in a family of five children but his father died when he was twelve, from wounds incurred when he was gassed in the First World War. I learnt from them both, though perhaps more from my mother who was more intellectual and better educated. She could play the piano nicely and she taught me to sing—we often sang when I was little and she was bathing me—'Blow the Wind Southerly', and 'Early One Morning' were the favourites.

One Sunday morning our father took my sister and me out. I know now it was an excuse to give us a surprise, for when we returned home he took us straight away into the living room where, in the middle of the floor were all ten volumes of Arthur Mee's *Children's Encyclopaedia*, surrounded by the track and rolling stock and engines of a clockwork train set. Funnily enough, I never took to the train set but I fell in love with the encyclopaedia. I devoured the volumes, read the stories they contained and was inspired by the history and the science.

Later, when I started secondary school, I was able to write the story of Attilla the Hun for my new history teacher, all learned from Arthur Mee. I learnt about the planets and the solar system, the stars and the natural world. It was truly a cornucopia of knowledge. I think it beats Wikipedia any time.

Holidays were an annual event. My father was never keen on them. For him, a holiday was time spent at home. My mother was the planner and the doer. We usually went to the West Country in a hired car. Every one of these expeditions was exciting, with the first day being marked by the first sighting of the sea. But two holidays were especially memorable. It was I think in 1955 that my mother first answered an advertisement in the *Daily Telegraph* (which my parents read every day) from a boarding house on the Isle of Wight. This turned out to be Mrs Cook's, a house which became a legend to my sister and me. We went by train to Portsmouth, then by ferry to the Isle, and onward by steam train (they all were steam in those days) to Horringford. Here we alighted and walked up a farm road to Mrs Cook's house. This was enormous by our standards and housed two or three families of holiday makers, who were given breakfast and dinner each day, as well as jugs of hot water in their rooms for washing and shaving.

Mrs Cook was nice and very proper. She thought nothing of making me a treacle tart for pudding, once she realised that I had not yet developed a taste for rhubarb, which everyone else had. Best of all, next door was the perfect farm—milking cows in a milking parlour, pigs in sties, ferrets in cages and chickens in a huge run. The farmer and his staff were friendly and we had the freedom of the farm yard. We were there every morning and evening. Our days were on the beach, at Sandown, Shanklin and elsewhere—anywhere we could reach on the Isle's rail network. It was magic. We went again the next year. I have never forgotten those short four weeks.

All this time we were getting bigger and older. Back in the real world my sister had taken her 11-plus examination and won a scholarship to Croydon High School, the top school for girls and a Girls Public Day School Trust school. She started there in 1954 and thrived.

I took my 11-plus in 1957. It was a very competitive exam and pupils succeeding in it were offered places in a range of schools, from the best in the area (mainly direct grant or independent but offering scholarships) to the less good. I was interviewed afterwards, presumably by representatives of schools that might be interested in me as a pupil. There was a text to read. It was about Dunkirk, the war again, of which I knew quite a lot. I was offered a place at Trinity School, part of the Whitgift Foundation. All seemed set for my future. But, as Harold Macmillan would have said, events intervened.

In 1956 post-war Britain endured its most humiliating moments, in the crisis over the Egyptian nationalisation of the Suez canal. The story is well known and I will not repeat it here but it had an unexpected effect on our family. I, a young boy, patriotic and ignorant of the world, followed the unfolding political and military drama with interest and enthusiasm. My parents, and especially my father, followed it with dismay and then despair. With an attitude that I saw later whenever my father noticed a Japanese car on the roads and remarked 'Who won the war anyway?', I heard him declare that Britain was over. The country was no longer the shining victor of the Second World War but a ruin. I was never sure who had ruined it.

The effect on him of Suez was profound and earth-shaking. He had just enjoyed a tremendous professional success. As a more or less self-taught draughtsman and engineer he had led a team at his company, Allen & Hanburys, which made medical equipment, in designing an operating table which was accepted into general service in the National Health Service.

The company had given him a handsome bonus which he used to buy our first car, a second-hand Hillman Minx. We also had a telephone installed. Now he decided to leave it all behind and announced that we should all move to Canada and start a new life in a country with a future. His younger brother Chris had already made the same decision in the hope of a better life, and I think this may have been very influential on my father.

The scale of this decision did not strike me at the time. I don't remember ever asking about my schooling or my sister's. I trusted my parents and was sure that it was all for the best and would work out well. It seemed exciting—and it was. Before we knew it, our house was sold, visas obtained, tickets bought and we were at the station to catch the train to Liverpool and embark on the RMS (Royal Mail Ship) *Carinthia*, a Cunard liner, to go to Montreal and thence to Vancouver for our new life. My father had no job to go to and we would have

With my mother on the RMS Carinthia in the St Lawrence Seaway, 1957.

to find somewhere to live but those minor matters did not seem important at the time.

We had a wonderful, sunny voyage out. On the approach to the St Lawrence Seaway we saw whales and icebergs. It was very exciting. But when we disembarked at Montreal there was a telegram from my father's brother Chris, who with his family had also just left for Canada. Chris had made his way to Vancouver, had found no work there and had headed back to Toronto in the hope of better luck. He advised us to do the same, so we changed plans and joined him there.

It was, I suppose a harbinger of things to come. At first we stayed in a cheap hotel near the main railway station. Then my parents found a basement flat to rent in an area of Toronto called Willowdale. My father got a job but somehow it didn't last longer than a week. He found no other work and after less than a month, with money haemorrhaging fast, my parents decided to return to London.

This was a momentous decision, throwing into question everything about the whole adventure, but again I trusted my parents and didn't wonder what on Earth was going on. My father flew back and we—my mother, sister and I—followed by sea two weeks later, on Canadian Pacific's *The Empress of France*. It was a greyer, colder voyage than the one out.

When we finally arrived in London my father told us that he had wondered why he had returned at all, once he saw the reality of ground-down, post-war Britain again. There was no turning back this time however. Fortunately my father's mother had obtained a council house on the big new post-war estate at New Addington, with enough room to put us all up for the time being. My father set about getting a job which proved surprisingly easy. My mother set about changing the family's fortunes by insisting that we left London and lived in the country. We ended up in a new house at East Grinstead in

Sussex, then a small country market town, and in September 1957 my sister and I started school again, at East Grinstead County Grammar School. It was a new beginning, though not what my father had envisaged. He named our new home 'Willowdale' after the area in Toronto we had lived in.

I suppose we should blame the war for all that happened to change our lives. My father felt that exhausted Britain was no place to bring up two children. He meant the best for us and goodness knows what torment he went through.

I think that in the end it all worked out for the best. My sister and I were happy and both did well. What more could we ask? We never again really talked about the Canada expedition and I certainly never criticised my parents for it, although I now see that it was, quite simply, a mistake.

A Teenager

At Winterbourne Junior School there had been a tarmac playground where, in the summer term, we played cricket against a chalked wicket on the wall at playtime. Occasionally we were taken to the local recreation ground to play football, but that was it, so far as sport was concerned. My first recollection of life at East Grinstead County Grammar School was sitting in the classroom looking out at acres of playing fields. I had never seen anything like it. I was not thought of as sporty but those playing fields would, in due course, affect me deeply.

In the meantime, I was settling into a new school where I knew no one—except my sister, for this was a co-educational school. I had no experience of girls, really, and was terribly shy; I could not talk to those in my class or even look them in the eye. I was better with the boys but not much. It took a long time to settle in and longer to establish myself. It was an asset to be relatively bright, so that at the end of the first term, when pupils were sorted out into streamed classes, I was in the top group, class 1A.

Secondary school was of course quite different from my junior school. Most excitingly we started sciences, foreign languages (French and Latin) and woodwork and metalwork. The latter were particularly attractive. It was true that, at home, I often helped my father in his workshop, where he had a bench and a vice, doing some job on our car or some woodwork project he had, but with him it was always 'Hold this, Bill' (his nickname for me). I was never allowed to do anything myself. Once I started practical studies in the school workshops, however, I wanted to do things myself—and so began a habit that has given a lifetime of pleasure.

As for the rest, I was never a scientist, in spite of a deep interest in and growing knowledge of the natural world, and languages were never my forte, though I ended up taking a dead language, Latin (which I found and still find to be very much alive) to A Level. Curiously, in spite of my ineptitude at languages, I also ended up learning two quite difficult languages that would prove useful for my profession and achieving a decent level of proficiency in both. So, don't ever believe that you can't do the impossible. You can. But my strengths lay elsewhere, in history and English, and also on the playing field.

The beginning of secondary school posed many problems for this almost adolescent boy. First of all, I had no friends, having left behind the few I had in Thornton Heath, so I went looking for friends. I had no idea that friendship was based on common interests and values, and it never occurred to me to ask what were my own interests were and what sort of people I might want as friends. At breaktime at school I would ask other boys in my class: will you be my best friend? I think they were mystified. They were nearly all from the town or surrounding villages and many had been at school with each other already. I was the odd one out.

Somehow I did make friends, first of all with Ron, with whom I am still very good friends. And I did find one other boy in a similar situation to mine. He stood out from the crowd as he was the tallest boy in our year and the only one in long trousers. His name was Tim and he came from a country estate in Ardingly, where his father was estate manager. His parents were much older than the parents of other boys of my age (Tim thought he was a mistake, arriving long after his sister and brother were born) and their house was isolated, so that, like me, Tim was looking for friends and company. It turns out that we are still friends today, have a great deal in common and see each other regularly. But I did not foresee that at that early, testing time.

The second problem was what was I interested in, if anything. I had been a cub and then a boy scout in Thornton Heath and had loved it, so I joined a local scout troop where I eventually became troop leader. That filled Friday evenings and sometimes a bit more of my free time. I also started to go fishing. My parents had for some unknown reason given me a fishing rod for my birthday one year. I had never shown any interest in fishing so it was a bit of a surprise. But here we were, in the countryside, with lakes and streams all around and the chance to use my tackle, and so I did. Indeed, fishing became a great passion. Moreover, I became seriously interested in fish and water life and read voraciously about them. I joined the local angling society and fished regularly and with some success, but nearly always returning my catch to the water. It is curious that, with the onset of puberty, and perhaps because I was developing real, deeper interests, I gradually fell out with both scouting and fishing. Girls, the youth club, pop music and sport replaced them. I also began to read seriously.

After the excitement of Arthur Mee I had started to read novels, especially Enid Blyton, Captain W.E. Johns (the Biggles books) but also Richard Jeffries and other, more difficult writers. As a teenager I began another, longer journey of properly exploring English literature. I realise now that this journey will never end but I am still enjoying it. I was guided by my mother, always a great reader and one who had read much modern American and British literature, and my sister, whose love of reading took her into the library often. She later became an accomplished librarian.

I was also compelled by school and the syllabus to read for exams. This led to Shakespeare and poetry, especially the romantics, and then to Milton. By the time I was in the sixth form I had discovered Dickens and Hardy. The dream of being invited to *Desert Island Discs* and having to choose that third book to accompany the *Bible* and *Shakespeare* started to haunt me. What should it be? *Paradise Lost*, I now usually conclude. But I am not sure. It is part of maturing and growing that you discover things that will stay with you all your life. The immense pleasure of reading remains.

In my second year at the grammar school I found, to everyone's astonishment, that I could run quite fast. By the time I left school my speed and fitness had got me into the senior rugby fifteen and the athletics team. I also, once, won the 440 yards (as it then was) in the school sports. I went on running into my forties, completing my last competitive race in Harare, Zimbabwe, in 1992 when I ran a ten-miler in 70 minutes, which I thought was not bad for a 46-year-old.

Sport, of course, was social. The chatter in the coach going to a Saturday away match was always special and was often about what we had seen the night before on *Ready, Steady, Go*, ITV's big pop-music show which broadcast on Friday evenings at 6 pm, with the proclamation that 'The Weekend Starts Here.' Being in the school rugby team raised one's profile and prestige more than being clever. Being given the rugby or athletics colours at the daily assembly was even better, since everyone, including the girls, saw you.

On Saturday night there was the Youth Club and, after it, a magic time when I would get out my old valve radio set, hook up the wire arial and get into bed to listen to David Jacobs host one of only two pop-music programmes then available on the

BBC's Light Programme, *Pick of the Pops* (the other was *Saturday Club* on Saturday mornings). It began at 10.15 pm and was formative in shaping my tastes. Funnily enough, I never listened to Radio Luxembourg, Radio Caroline or the other pirate radio stations that were then coming on the air, whose popularity eventually forced the BBC to set up Radio 1.

And so to girls. I was so shy as a teenager that I could barely bring myself to talk even to the fifteen young women with whom I shared a classroom. It also seemed a taboo issue at home, where my parents were shocked if I expressed any curiosity about girls or sex. I realise now that for my mother and father the relationship they had was probably their only relationship and one that started quite late in their adolescent lives. They too were shy about these things. I had no sex education, apart from a one-minute talk from my father one Sunday evening during the interval in *Sunday Night at the London Palladium*, an ITV staple which we always watched. My sister and mother must have left the room to make tea so my father seized the opportunity to tell me the facts of life. Well, in a fashion. I was little wiser after this.

Eventually I did find a girlfriend and then two more before I left school. But girls were never my strong point. How I envied boys who found it easier. Some, indeed, found it very easy and went, as they used to say, all the way. I think that that was unusual at the time—this was only the beginning of the age of sexual liberation and the pill, and East Grinstead was a very conservative place (there was a public row when it was revealed that the local dance hall had installed a condom vending machine in the men's toilets). And some boys got their girlfriends into trouble—and at that time it was very definitely trouble.

One event that I now find shocking occurred in my last year of school. At morning assembly the headmaster announced that a boy in the lower sixth, who happened to be a neighbour of ours, had been expelled with his younger girlfriend, who was also at the school, because she was pregnant. It was a terrible thing to do to them; and worse, the girl's parents refused to help her and threw her out of their house. The pair got married and stayed together for a while but their young lives were shattered. It probably wouldn't happen now. But this was 1964, a quite different world. It was only much later that my parents, who had always told us that they had married in 1941, revealed that they had in fact married in 1942, with my mother expecting my sister. They had felt that we should not know this.

In spite of the condom vending machine (I don't remember ever seeing it and in any case I didn't know what a condom was), the local dance hall was a place I started to go to regularly. They hosted a lot of the popular bands of my youth. I have magic memories of seeing the sixties bands the Kinks and Manfred Mann there, in a half-empty hall, and dancing with my friend Tim as there did not seem to be any girls to dance with. Perhaps they didn't want to dance with us—who knows?

It was after one such evening in 1963 that I got home to find my parents waiting for me, very excited. While I was out, my headmaster had telephoned to say that he had appointed me as head boy of the school. I was nonplussed by this and really did not know how to deal with it. Looking back, I know that there had been stronger candidates but I think the staff had been in disagreement and that I was the compromise. At any rate, that is how I explain it, as I was certainly not the right person: I was immature and lacking in confidence, and I struggled to understand the role. I have to say, the Head gave me no guidance at all about what he expected from me. Later on, being head boy looked good on my CV, once I had one, but I could have done without this challenge. I really needed to concentrate on my studies, where things were not going well.

Typical of my attitude was an incident in October 1962. The world was watching with bated breath the clash between the USA and the Soviet Union over the latter's secret but now exposed decision to deploy nuclear missiles to Cuba, missiles that had the range to reach almost any target in the USA. In one of our A-level history lessons I asked our teacher, Miss Edwards, a sweet, elderly dear of a woman, if she thought there would be a war. There was of course a real risk of that and the Royal Air Force was on full alert with its V-bomber force at a few minutes' readiness for take-off. Miss Edwards then spent the rest of the lesson talking about the Cuba crisis. My real reason for asking was not any profound interest in Cuba but my wish to avoid another lesson on nineteenth century European history. I was quite sure that Miss Edwards would rise to the bait and I was right.

The fact was, I was not seriously engaged in the history I was studying, nor was I reading outside the immediate exam curriculum. I was however deeply interested in politics and international affairs, so perhaps my question was not just a time-waster. And the shadow of war really did hang over us all the time and in its own way affected me deeply. I went on to join the Campaign for Nuclear Disarmament (CND) and took part in one of the annual marches from Aldermaston to London, calling for disarmament. You might say that was a result. My history did not however improve.

While I was at grammar school something happened at home that was very sad and caused great unhappiness. In about 1960 my father, whose employer made hospital sterilisers, and who was doing very well, was headhunted by an American company, Amsco (the American Steriliser Company) to set up a subsidiary in Britain. It offered him a lot more money than he was getting and he, understandably, took the job. This took him away, first to the USA to meet the Amsco executives, and then to exhibitions of hospital equipment in Britain. Our mother hated this and eventually had a breakdown and was taken into hospital for two weeks. My father's mother, Ma, came to look after us all while Mum was away. When she returned I think she found it very difficult to get back to normal, and over time we all noticed her mental stability deteriorating. Typically, my father's job with Amsco came to nothing, as the company withdrew from the British market, and soon he was out of work. He never worked in the hospital equipment business again, his reputation in it having been ruined by this episode. After a brief attempt at running his own photographic business he made his living with a company that made small steel furnaces. It was sad. He could have done so much better.

University

Once I got into the upper-sixth form at East Grinstead County Grammar, I applied for a place at university, like many of my fellow pupils. This was quite an achievement. If successful I would be the first person in our wider family to go to university. I was already the first to stay on to the sixth form. I don't recall ever thinking about this at the time because university just seemed the natural next step. But for nearly all of us, just applying was a big thing, and an even bigger thing if it came off.

As it happens, I applied for and was offered a place at a couple of universities, Southampton and Hull, 'red brick' as they were called, in contrast to the dreaming spires of Oxford and Cambridge. I wanted to read English and Latin, a joint studies degree which promised a wide education, although I had given no thought to what I might do when I graduated. One step at a time!

In the event I did so badly at A level that neither place materialised. Today pupils expect and are expected to get 3 As or A stars. I got a B, a C and a D, having not taken the exams seriously enough and not given them the effort they deserved. What should I do? I had to think fast. Finally, I enrolled at what was then Kingston Technical College to do a London University external degree. I got quite far down the road of preparing for this, including finding digs to live in.

Then, later that summer, about two weeks before I was to start at Kingston, I was at home preparing lunch for my parents, who had gone shopping. A large envelope fell through our letter box. It was an offer of a place at a proper university, at Cardiff, part of the University of Wales then, to read for an arts degree. This had come through the central clearing scheme, set up to match students with places that universities wanted to fill. I accepted at once. I applied for a grant to cover my costs and, since these were means tested and my parents were not well off, was given a full maintenance grant, with all my fees paid.

It should have been exciting but I was nervous and not prepared for tertiary education. My friend Tim rang me the night before he and I were both to travel to our new college lives (he went off to Strathclyde University in Glasgow). Tim was full of eagerness to leave home and be independent and take on the world and he asked if I was excited. I wasn't, just apprehensive, but off I went. After a rocky start I had an experience that changed me and helped to determine what happened next.

In one way only was I ready for university life: I was intellectually curious and keen to read and to learn. I sat in the university library, a wonderful Victorian building, in my first week and thought to myself: gosh, I am so lucky to be here. And indeed I was, though I could have made more of my first and second years. An early setback was my failure to get into the college's rugby teams. At that time I played either on the wing or in the centre, where my speed counted more than my (slight) size. At the trials I found myself playing scrum half, a position I had never played in. I was no good at it and I did not get, or have the nerve to demand, a second chance.

Sport had been so important to me at school that I found it hard not to be able to enjoy on a regular organised basis but that is what happened. It would have made a difference socially too. The only people I met thereafter were those in the classes I was taking and at the Saturday Night Hop. Nor did I join any of the many student societies and clubs that would have made life so much more enjoyable and interesting. For the first two years I just worked, studying furiously and not really making any friends.

I ran regularly, and stayed slim and fit, but I was not a happy young man and lived in a hall of residence which I actively disliked. It was only at the end of my second year that I decided to take charge of my life. I moved out of hall and into digs with a Mrs Steele, a lovely elderly lady who lived with her husband in a terraced house in Roath Park, a Cardiff suburb. I shared with a fellow named Bob, whose girlfriend Mary was often there too. They became good friends and we spent many a night in the local pub. Probably for the first time at Cardiff I was content; and in that frame of mind I began to work methodically and read constructively.

I had in the end opted for a degree in history. The History Department was, rather to my surprise, quite distinguished, with a number of well-known historians on the team. It also offered an unusually good course, covering not just the staple diet of British and European history but also the history of the Far East, of the USA, of science, of economics and of philosophy. I found it fascinating and buried myself in it. I also started playing football and going to the university gym (an incredible, free facility) regularly. I was Mr Fitness, something which stayed with me, whatever I did, in future life.

In this contented way, I worked myself to a first-class honours degree, the only one in history that year. After the misery of A level failure in 1964, this was a big moment but I did not have a clue what to do next: the one-step-at-a-time approach persisted. Fortunately, perhaps, the decision was rather taken out of my hands. On the day that our professor and head of the History Department announced our results to an apprehensive group of students sitting in the Junior Common Room, our lecturer in modern European history was also present. He approached me and asked if I would like to do a doctorate under his supervision. Of course I said yes.

What happened after that was both good and bad. I had spent the summer working on a farm in Sussex, enjoying myself immensely before going to southern Italy for a holiday with Tim and another friend from school. I returned to Cardiff to start work on my doctorate in October, feeling pretty good about the world and with a new-found self-confidence.

The first thing I had to do was to decide what would be the subject of my thesis. As an undergraduate I had developed an interest in Central and Eastern Europe and was moved by the struggles for independence of those nations that were carved out of the great nineteenth-century European empires, and indeed by the Russian Revolution of 1917. So I looked to something linked to these events. I thought I had found something promising, to do with the creation of Yugoslavia, and began to work on this.

All this was in Cardiff, where other good things began to happen. As a postgraduate I began to meet other postgrads, who were, not surprisingly, interesting and intelligent people. I went to parties and lunches and enjoyed the sort of conversations I had expected but never found as an undergraduate. I was changing and maturing and slowly becoming a man. It was a good time.

Then I moved to London to begin my proper research, mainly at the Public Records Office (then in Chancery Lane in central London). I took a flat in Kennington with an old friend from Cardiff who was training in local government and I set to work. In one way I enjoyed the challenge of hard intellectual work, be it reading documents at the PRO or researching in one of the specialist libraries that I had access to. On the other I found I was desperately lonely. A lot of the structure of life in Cardiff had gone. There was no football and no gym to slip into for an hour. I hardly knew a soul and discovered that research is a very solitary business, or so it was for me. The Kennington flat didn't help really. We had no bathroom, just a shared outside toilet, and no proper kitchen. Once a week my flatmate and I went to the local public baths where, for six pence, you could have half an hour in a bath full of very hot water. Even so, it was all a bit primitive and the flat was very cold in the winter. Weekends there were particularly grim.

But worse was to come. One day I went to see the professor of modern European history at the LSE, a very distinguished professor called James Joll, and he told me he was supervising a student who was working on the same subject as I was. This should not have happened but it was my mistake as I had started much later than this other fellow and should have found his subject registered on the system that existed to avoid this sort of clash. In the end I went to meet him and read what he had so far written. It covered all the territory that I planned to write about. I thought hard about what to do. There was nothing to stop me starting again. But I decided not to and called a halt to the whole project. It was really a relief. I was not cut out for research or the academic life. I wanted something different. The question was, what?

Being in London and seeing all those people on the streets going to work had already made me start thinking that I would like a job. With hindsight I could have become a builder or a bar manager. Student life had brought me into contact with both these professions and I was probably quite well qualified for either. During my first long summer vacation I worked as a labourer for a local building firm in East Grinstead. I was young and fit and ready to do anything, so I dug holes and trenches, mixed concrete, and pushed wheelbarrows of it for, it seemed, miles. I quite enjoyed it and I certainly learned things that I still draw on today, so it was very good experience.

One the other hand I found much of it monotonous and I longed for the breaks (what was called lunch at 11 am and then dinner at 1 pm, with a short tea break in the afternoon) when I could read my book. I also met people of a type I had not really encountered before: hard-working but poorly educated, and a bit suspicious of a bloke who read the *Times* (still in its historic format with adverts and notices on the front page) each day. The foreman used to ask how my shares were doing. I didn't have any, of course.

And then there was the Star Inn at Felbridge. With two years of working weekends as a sixth former at the upmarket Old Felbridge Hotel at East Grinstead, I did know a bit about being a barman. But little prepared me for serving in the public bar at the Star when I started there in the summer of 1966. In those days there were two, maybe three, bars in a pub: usually at least a public and a saloon bar. They were differentiated by the price of drinks and the comfort of the surroundings; also, I suppose, by the type of people who used them. The Star's public bar had sawdust on the floor and only hard seats. Some of the customers were pretty hard too. There were some challenging moments, as once when a customer, not satisfied with the half pint I had given him, leaned over the bar and topped it up himself. It was expected that I would know what each person drank and it was my job to refill empty glasses.

Sometimes customers would bang a penny (the pre-decimalization sort, so quite large) on the counter to demand attention. They didn't speak to me to explain what they wanted. I had to know. Please and thank-you were rare. Again, experience. The landlord was ex-army (non-commissioned

At the Old Felbridge Hotel with barmaids Wynn and Christine, 1963.

officer) and had an eye for the girls. In the end he got one of the barmaids into trouble (that expression again) and his wife threw him out and he went off with the girl. I had known her slightly and felt sorry that here was another life wrecked.

Anyway, with all of that behind me, it was perhaps a good decision that I decided to look for an office job, though with little idea of what this meant or what I would enjoy, let alone be good at.

Work

When I started working I met people, young men like me, who were driven by ambition, by a huge determination to do very well, by the desire to be wealthy. Some were soon plotting their whole career and knew exactly in what role, and with what honours (a knighthood was much coveted in the civil service) they wished to end up. As I entered the world of employment, I had no such thoughts. I wanted to pay the bills, of course, but I had no plan for my life, no thoughts really beyond today. Nor did I have anyone who encouraged me to think more constructively, more long term. It was enough that I was no longer a student, that I wanted a job of some sort. I would have driven a truck or, better, become a guide for London's growing tourist industry, if necessary. It did not seem to me to be important. That was of course a mistake and led me into two jobs for which I was not suited and where I didn't stay very long.

I had other things on my mind too. I was meeting people in London and I was reading widely, discovering authors like Lawrence Durrell and James Joyce and attending poetry readings, even once to a concrete poetry recital (it was awful). I was going to concerts and beginning that long and wonderful journey from the world of pop to the world of classical music.

There were also, occasionally, girls. Looking back I can see that I had few real friends and lacked any framework in which to start building my life. Most of all I was discontented with my first jobs and increasingly wanted something that would grip and occupy and satisfy me. I wasn't looking for glamour or adventure, though in due course I would get a bit of both.

I talked to my sister about this. At that time she was the librarian in a big school in Crawley and worked with a teacher with whom she had become friendly. This woman was married to a senior civil servant, and—out of the blue—they invited me for coffee one Sunday morning, to talk about my future. My sister and I arrived and were given coffee, and then I was despatched into the garden, where the husband was digging his vegetable patch. He asked me what I was interested in. I said international affairs, politics, Central and Eastern Europe. He said, 'You should apply for the Foreign Office.' I was staggered. Such a thought had never crossed my mind, nor that of my parents. We didn't know people who had jobs in organisations like that. In fact we didn't know anyone in the civil service and my parents' closest friends were the chap who owned the local cycle shop and a teacher Dad had been at school with before the war. I went away to think about this, with the offer from my sister's friend's husband (who hardly knew me) of a reference.

Not only did I know no one in the Foreign Office, I knew almost nothing about what it did, what was required of its staff and what sort of life they led, so to apply would be a big gamble. But I did. I was bored and frustrated and perhaps I had the beginning of the idea that life had more to offer than I was getting.

The application process meant applying for the Civil Service Fast Stream, as it then was. I quickly discovered that my First Class degree was a huge advantage: it meant I did not have to take the preliminary exams. The assumption was that I was bright enough to go straight to the main selection process. In

September 1968 I duly presented myself at the Civil Service Commission, then in Savile Row in central London. There were about 25 candidates, for all the civil service departments. We were put through a gruelling two days of tests, interviews and exercises. It was fun and I was with a group of intelligent and interesting young people. At the end we went our separate ways and I only saw one of them again, a rather attractive young woman whom I took out for a while until she met someone who offered her more.

It was a time of waiting. I had applied for the Foreign Office and then, a second choice, the Ministry of Defence. I had no plan for failure if neither turned up. I cannot remember how long the wait was but one day I got home from work to find a letter offering me a place in HM Diplomatic Service, so the Foreign Office it was. I was delighted. Life, perhaps, was beginning to take off. I remember meeting some of my friends that evening in a pub and telling them. They seemed unimpressed. In contrast my parents were impressed, as indeed was my old school. (My mother was by that time the school bursar and told the head and others. I think they found it hard to believe.)

My next concern was how to start my new career as soon as possible. Here there was a snag. The Foreign Office had an annual intake of fast-stream entrants who began work in September each year with a set induction course and proper training and so on. I didn't fit into that timing and when it was suggested that I wait, I pressed to be admitted earlier, if at all possible. In the end the Office invited me to start on 20 January 1969. I duly handed in my resignation, with a month's notice, to my then employer, who immediately cancelled the Christmas bonus they had awarded me. Oh dear. I wasn't that bothered, though—just excited and looking forward to ... I didn't really know what.

A New World

When I first entered the Foreign Office's grand buildings between Downing Street and King Charles Street in Whitehall, I embarked on a journey that was to last 34 years, take me to six overseas postings and a variety of interesting jobs at home, and bring me close to some great people and even greater events. I started as a humble and rather overawed third secretary in the Office in London and finished my career as Her Majesty's Ambassador to Hungary. I worked with some extraordinary people. I saw huge changes in the world and in Britain's place

Starting at the Foreign and Commonwealth Office in 1969, aged 23.

in it, not least Britain's joining the European Economic Community (later the European Union) and so strengthening its position in the world as well as in Europe (fortunately I had no hand in its departure in 2020). I was also there for the decay and collapse of the Soviet empire in Eastern Europe, the effort to build liberal, free-market democracies in the states that emerged afterwards, and 9/11 and the preoccupation with Islamic terrorism that followed.

The Diplomatic Service was itself transformed during my time. Equal opportunities legislation brought to an end the rule that a female member had to resign on marriage, and so opened up the service for women to have fulfilling careers. Technological change was also revolutionary. Communications for the Warsaw embassy in 1970 meant an ex-Navy radio operator who tapped out our reports in Morse Code. By the time I left, computers and digital communications had arrived. I look back with a wry smile at the room where I worked in 1969, including the bell we pressed to summon more coal for the open fire in winter, and at the leisurely departmental coffee and tea breaks, and at the daily starting time of 10 am. In my last London job I started at 7 am and rarely left before 7 at night. Another change, sadly, was that in 1969 I could walk up Downing Street and into the Foreign Office without hindrance. The IRA and then Al-Qaeda put an end to all that. Like many senior diplomats I lived with guards for the last years of my career.

The work was demanding, pressured and endless. I got used to working late in the evening and sometimes weekends. In the 1980s when I was dealing with South Africa, I made the mistake of living quite near the Office in London and could easily drive in to sort out a Sunday emergency. As a result the resident clerks quickly learned that I was the fellow to phone when problems cropped up.

In 1969, when I started, I was in many ways an outsider in the Diplomatic Service. The service tended to recruit its fast streamers from Oxbridge graduates, who had usually been to public (independent) schools. It was unusual to take in someone who had a different background. I don't think that ever counted against me, except in two respects. Firstly, my colleagues, to a man and woman, enjoyed the self-confidence which the independent schools cultivate so well. I never developed that. Indeed I think it has to be acquired at school. They also found it easier to network, something that was alien to me.

But I enjoyed the highly intellectual world of the service, its high demands and its collegiality, something I missed when, at the end of my working life, I spent four years at Vodafone. Standards were high. As one of my first and best managers said to me after reading something I had written, 'there is only one standard'—he meant *excellence*, which I had fallen short of. When I failed in the Foreign Office, it was through my own failings, not the attitude of others. Likewise where I succeeded, it was because I had got things right, assembled the right arguments, reached the right conclusion, given correct advice or taken the right decision.

The lifestyle was strange and challenging in its own way. London-based life was, I suppose, quite normal for any busy executive. The pattern of postings (I spent half of my career overseas) was also familiar to those who worked for large multinationals. It was nonetheless a far cry from the settled, steady lives of the boys I had been at school with and when later I talked to them about it they found it strange that I did not live in the same place for more than three or four years at a time.

I certainly missed out on being part of a community, and perhaps on things like watching a garden grow. Instead I was in houses I didn't own and had not chosen for myself, often with servants I was ill-equipped to manage, look after and occasionally discipline. Gardens were for the gardener.

My last diplomatic home was a neo-baroque palace in the nicest suburb of Budapest, with a bevy of staff and wonderful rooms and furniture with modern British masterpieces on the walls. I never came to like it. Indeed, living a private life there was hard and was only achieved on a few occasions when I left the official residence and escaped for a weekend in, say, Vienna. It was similar in Warsaw where official life was very busy and only made palatable by getting away to a cottage I had rented for the summer at Różan in north-east Poland.

I did not know any of this when I started. I think others, some from diplomatic families whose fathers had been ambassadors, were better prepared. But anyway, there was a lot that was new, and had to be adjusted to, and learned and understood. Most of all I had to learn what the Foreign Office and its embassies did, how they did it, and how everything meshed together.

Over time most officers establish a reputation among their colleagues. I think I achieved this, though perhaps a little later than others. My strength, though I am not sure this was recognised very well, was that I spent half of my career dealing with Communist and then post-Communist Eastern and Central Europe, an experience probably unique in the Diplomatic Service at that time. At one time, when I was head of the Office's Central European Department, I knew every prime minister, president and foreign minister in the region. This was in the 1990s, when Britain played a key role in the reconstruction of those countries as they emerged from Soviet domination. That was the best job I ever had. I had more influence on policy than at any other time, even when I was an ambassador myself. On the other hand, I never worked in a major embassy such as Washington or Paris, where the high fliers of the service rub shoulders and get to know each other. It meant that I never developed a network of any strength or use.

People often ask me which of my postings was the best? I always say that I enjoyed them all. There is, after all, no point in being somewhere for two or three or more years and not enjoying it. Everywhere has something to offer, of interest, of pleasure, of excitement.

In Zimbabwe I not only spent weeks in the bush, watching animals and birds, but also had the privilege of planning, and taking part in, a state visit by the Queen (*see pages* 55–57). Everywhere there were people to meet and get to know, both as contacts who would be useful to you in the way you did your job or as friends. Sometimes these came together, as in Poland in the late 1980s when we were working closely with the (illegal) opposition movement, Solidarity.

The intellectual interest of different places did of course vary, some being more important to the audience in London than others. For example, although life in Bangladesh was very tough, I treasure the two years I spent there, just after that very poor and insignificant country gained independence from Pakistan, even though nobody in London had any interest at all in the country except for the issues raised by immigration. I made some wonderful friends among the Bengalis I met and learnt so much about a totally different culture, as well as having experiences like flying up country in a single-engine plane and landing on the cricket pitch at the country's police academy. All in all, a rich and fulfilling life. I was fortunate to have it.

My mother was always in two minds about my career. She did not really understand what I was doing, which didn't help; and while she recognised that it was prestigious and impressed her friends, part of her wanted me to be living just around the corner and doing something 'normal' like being a bricklayer. I wasn't, though, and when I tried something else, after I left the Office, I was, in truth, a fish out of water.

So much of what I did brought me into touch with the war, in whose shadow I had started my life. One of the first, challenging tasks given to me in 1969 was to recommend whether anyone from Britain should attend the funeral of the Soviet Marshal Voroshilov, one of Stalin's leading generals in the fight against Nazi Germany.

In Poland the war loomed large in both my postings. Poland was of course home to many of the concentration camps of the Holocaust and I occasionally took visitors to the terrible camp at Majdanek, nearer to Warsaw than was Auschwitz in the south, to see for themselves the remains of that appalling time. Almost everywhere I lived there were Commonwealth war

With Polish President Aleksander Kwaśniewski at the Budapest Commonwealth War Cemetery, before laying a wreath to honour Polish RAF aircrew killed flying to supply the Warsaw uprising of 1944. Spring 2003.

cemeteries, and in Hungary I accompanied the president of Poland Aleksander Kwaśniewski when he visited the Budapest cemetery in which lay the remains of Royal Air Force crew, including Poles, who had lost their lives flying from Italy to Warsaw to drop supplies to the insurgents in the uprising against the Germans in August 1944.

In 1994 I recommended that Prime Minister John Major should go to Warsaw to attend the commemoration of the fiftieth anniversary of this tragic event. I accompanied him and briefed him on the plane on what had happened. And in 1993 I organised and attended the repatriation to Poland of the remains of General Sikorski, the Polish wartime leader who had died in an air crash in Gibraltar in 1943. The Polish aircraft that took the exhumed remains back to Warsaw was escorted out of British air space by two RAF Tornado fighter jets. It was a dramatic and nostalgic occasion. So the war was ever present, not just in my parents' recollections but in the things I was doing and experiencing.

Central Europe

I spent 34 years in the Foreign Office, at home and abroad. I had an unusual, some might say a modest, career. Although I never worked in one of Britain's large embassies, the posts I served in were not insignificant. Each was important in its own way, but only one, Communist Poland, really grabbed the attention of London. Not everybody saw its importance, of course. When I tried to explain what was happening in Poland in 1988 to one junior minister (David Mellor) he was dismissive. He was misguided, because Poland was leading the way to the fall of Communism. But there we are.

Over my six postings abroad and a number of home jobs I developed two strands of specialisation. The lesser of these was Southern Africa, with jobs at home and in Africa bringing me in touch with South African apartheid and those struggling against it, and the battle of an independent Zimbabwe to build a sound political and economic system. The greater strand was Communism in Central Europe and its aftermath. Indeed, it was this that I strived to make the centrepiece of my career, spending about half of my 34 years as a diplomat working on this theme.

It was Poland, my first posting, that in many ways dominated my thinking and where in the late 1980s, on a second posting, I had probably the most fun in my life overseas. When I was posted to the embassy in Warsaw in 1970,

I was a gauche and nervous young man, not speaking Polish well and not at all sure of himself or his role. I was rather overwhelmed by it all, and not least by the elite team that I joined there, all of them public-school (including my first Harrovian) and basically Oxbridge (though the Harrovian had gone to Trinity College Dublin). The Ambassador, Nicko Henderson, was a star in the Foreign Office and knew it.

I was lost at first and struggled to find my feet. I was helped by a sympathetic manager and then by my own determination to master my role and establish myself. I was also helped by events. Poland had seemed dull when I arrived in the summer that year but it exploded in December as protests against the policies of the Communist government (especially increases in the price of basic foodstuffs) broke out in the northern cities of Gdansk, Gdynia and Sopot. Suddenly London started to take notice and there were definitely interesting things to discover and understand.

In many ways my job became journalistic but there were barriers: the nature of the Communist system, the closed society, the tight control of the media, the firm grip on the population—all these made getting to the heart of what was happening very difficult. This was pre-internet, pre-mobile phone and pre-satellite TV: a different world. Our contact with Poles was very restricted and we learnt of the riots in the north from the BBC World Service, not from our contacts.

The protests in the north were suppressed brutally but it wasn't long before Communist leader Władysław Gomułka had a stroke and there was an internal party coup. Edward Gierek, a man who unusually read *Le Monde* every morning (he had spent the war in France as a miner on forced labour) took over. He brought in a new team and we needed to work out who they were, what they stood for and how they fitted into the political spectrum in so far as we understood it.

Meanwhile further protests broke out, this time in different Polish cities. In January 1971 I was despatched to Szczecin, in the northwest, to find out whatever I could about the strikes there and what the strikers wanted. I managed to get hold of a copy of their demands, which were mainly about food prices but also included the call for free trade unions, instead of the state-run ones that then existed. This was of course the harbinger of things to come and the formation of the Solidarity Trade Union in 1980.

I spent the next eighteen months watching the buying off of the population and the restoration of order. But I was confident that the dissatisfaction of the working class would not die away, in spite of the regime's measures to build more flats, produce more cars and offer Coca Cola to the masses (they bought a licence to produce this and I reported that some party hardliners were finding it hard to swallow).

I left Poland in the autumn of 1972 with a heavy heart. I had enjoyed my job and my time and learned a lot. I wasn't sure I would ever return and the future seemed bleak. I flirted with a change of career but this came to nothing and in the end I went off to Bangladesh for what was a quite different experience. But I did return to Warsaw eventually, in 1985, when I went back as Deputy Head of Mission. I was thrilled. The country I returned to had changed immensely, I felt. It had gone through further years of protest which eventually led to the formation and recognition of Solidarity and then its suppression with the imposition in December 1981 of martial law. But Solidarity lived on underground. Poles everywhere had also been inspired by the election of a Polish pope, John Paul II, the former bishop of Krakow, Karol Wojtyła, in 1978. The country seemed more open, less beaten down, even though there was even less, as far as I could see, in the shops.

My job had changed. I was the deputy CEO of a quite large

enterprise with many different functions, keeping an eye on some but with clear management and leadership functions for others. I tried to ensure that I did all the administrative work that was expected of me but I could not help being fascinated by the politics. By this time Mikhail Gorbachev had taken over in Moscow and there seemed a real prospect of change for the better in the Soviet Union but what did that mean for Poland? I gave my team authority to establish and develop contacts with all the opposition movements that existed (there were more than one) but in particular with Solidarity, in spite of its being banned. The Foreign Secretary encouraged this and our ambassador, John Morgan, decided that we should make contact, the first since martial law, with its leader Lech Wałęsa.

I accordingly arranged, in what I thought was great secrecy, a meeting in Gdansk and we drove up there for the occasion. After checking in at our hotel in Sopot we set off on a damp and dark evening to find the house of Wałęsa's priest, Father Henryk Jankowski, where our meeting was to take place. Perhaps inevitably I got lost and stopped to check the map, A car drove up beside us and the driver said to me, 'Follow me!' It was the Polish Security Police who knew all about our visit.

When we arrived at the venue for the meeting, Wałęsa was waiting anxiously outside, obviously wondering where we had got to. Once there we were joined by one of Solidarity's leading intellectual advisers, Tadeusz Mazowiecki. When he arrived Wałęsa introduced him with the words 'Here is Pan Tadeusz', a reference to a famous Polish poem by Adam Mickiewicz. The meeting was without substance but nonetheless important symbolically. I remember Morgan being unimpressed by Wałęsa but he left Poland shortly afterwards and our contacts with Solidarity continued.

Of course, I did other things than politics. In a rather bizarre episode, I tried to solve the problem of the embassy's złoty (Polish currency) mountain. This had accumulated because of our inability to spend the złoties that flowed in from visa fees or to convert this money into sterling, as the złoty was not convertible. I devised a plan to buy large quantities of bottled beetroot which would be sold by a Polish businessman in Britain. The proceeds would be in sterling and would accrue to the British government. It all seemed promising but the Polish authorities would not play the game and turned us down.

These and other activities kept me very busy. But our fascination with Solidarity was to reach its climax in late 1988, at a time when, while Gorbachev's reforms continued in the Soviet Union, Poland appeared to sink further into poverty and into two separate societies, the governing and the governed—although it was clear that some of those in the former group shared the despair felt by just about everyone in the latter group.

It was in September 1988 that, while in charge of the embassy during a hiatus between ambassadors, I received instructions from London to explore the possibility of a visit by Prime Minister Margaret Thatcher to Poland. She wanted to see Polish leader Wojciech Jaruzelski but also to go to Gdansk and meet Wałęsa. The initial Polish response was that Mrs Thatcher would be most welcome but that a meeting with the Solidarity leader was out of the question. I reported this and the message came back that the visit would not therefore take place. Deadlock. Then, at one of those diplomatic receptions I always hated, I ran into a Jaruzelski advisor, Colonel Wiesław Górnicki, formerly a rather distinguished journalist but latterly a close supporter of martial law and Solidarity's suppression. I had known him since my first posting, had time for him and was not unhappy to see him. But I was very surprised when he said how much the Poles were looking forward to seeing Mrs Thatcher, and of course she could go to Gdansk, providing she fulfilled one or two official engagements there. The Poles had decided that it was better to have Mrs T on these terms than not at all. So the scene was set for what proved to be an historic visit.

It fell to me and my team to arrange the visit. The Poles were very cooperative, as was Wałęsa, who left the guest list for the big lunch we arranged largely to me. By the time Mrs Thatcher touched down in the RAF VC10 aircraft at Warsaw's Okęcie airport, things had moved on in Poland's politics, indeed in Central Europe as a whole. Jaruzelski was now planning what were called Round Table talks with the legal opposition but he intended Wałęsa to be part of a group of Catholic intellectuals who would take part. So when Mrs Thatcher met Wałęsa, in a Gdansk very excited by her visit and very stage-managed by Solidarity, this became the central issue for him: should he accept the invitation or was it a trap to discredit him? Mrs Thatcher was clear: he should say Yes.

It was curious that there was little else discussed and other than Wałęsa, only one of the Solidarity team spoke: Bronisław Geremek. The others, who included some very clever people and some tough trade unionists, seemed too scared to intervene. (They told me afterwards that Wałęsa had told them not to speak.) Anyway, Wałęsa took Mrs Thatcher's advice, and less than a year later, and two months before the fall of the Berlin Wall, there were elections in which Solidarity did very well and the Communists very badly. Jaruzelski saw the writing on the wall and appointed Mazowiecki, the Pan Tadeusz of the 1985 meeting, as prime minister, the first non-Communist since 1948.

Communism in Poland was now in its death throes. What we didn't know was that Gorbachev had long ago told the Central-European Communist leaders that the Soviet Union would never again intervene to bail them out, as it had in

Photo courtesy of Associated Newspapers Ltd.

Prime Minister Thatcher meets Solidarity Leader Lech Wałęsa in Gdansk, 1988. Press Secretary Bernard Ingham and I are in the background.

Hungary in 1956 and in Czechoslovakia in 1968. This effectively pulled the rug from under their feet, as they lacked any real political legitimacy.

It was a wonderful time to be in Poland. I was also very lucky with my colleagues in Warsaw at this time. It was a great team, both the embassy and the British Council. Those of us involved in the Thatcher visit still, I think, regard this as the most exciting event we dealt with, a moment of history and a step in the rewriting of Central European politics. When Mrs Thatcher died in 2013 we all got together for a commemorative dinner, recalling that extraordinary visit to Gdansk.

Sadly, I was not around to witness the next chapter in this saga as the Foreign Office, in its wisdom, posted me to Zimbabwe and I missed it all. Worse still, I was completely cut off from any real news and could not follow it all. But I was determined to resume my Central-European career once I returned to London.

The opportunity duly turned up. I had gone back to London in 1992 with no job to go to, but by this time the Foreign Office had decided on a more competitive postings system and we were allowed to choose which jobs to apply for. The position of head of Central European Department was coming up and I resisted pressure to take other jobs so that I could hold out for this. I was lucky enough to be successful. So it was that I started what I regard as the best job of my career. Of course, I still wasn't very senior but I was the person who recommended to ministers what our policy in Central Europe should be.

The main framework of that had been set earlier, after the collapse of Communism and the Soviet Union. There was a shared Western goal: to ensure that the newly liberated Central European states became countries and societies like ours—liberal with a small L, capitalist, democratic and of course political allies and not enemies, as in the past. These objectives were also those of the successor regimes, generally speaking, though there were question marks over Romania. More generally, democracy for all these countries was a huge experiment and one of which they had little or no experience. There was lots to do but also enough money and political will to do it.

One major distraction was the break-up of Yugoslavia, which took place simultaneously and sucked away ministerial attention and energy. But we, and our partners in the European Union and Nato, pressed on. I not only worked in my rather splendid office in the Foreign Office building in Whitehall but travelled extensively, on my own or accompanying a minister, getting to know all the countries I was responsible for and meeting their presidents, prime ministers and other senior players. I had tremendous access, not because I was Nigel Thorpe, but because I represented the British government and we had weight, we counted, and were regarded everywhere as a serious player.

I did this job for four years. There were events that were significant, not least to me, like the repatriation of General Sikorski's remains (see Chapter 5) or the fiftieth anniversary of the Warsaw Uprising. There were also very difficult questions, such as our relationship with Russia and the challenge of building a constructive relationship with those difficult people while also responding to the security concerns of the former Soviet satellites, who all feared Russia and were suspicious of its long-term intentions towards them. This was acute in the Baltic states, whose occupation by the Soviets had involved the settlement in their countries of thousands of Russians who stayed on after 1991, and indeed had nowhere else to go, but were viewed by the newly independent states as a fifth column. I am not sure we ever got this right.

I advocated early entry into Nato for at least the Poles, Hungarians and Czechs, and also early membership of the EU for these three and the Baltic states as well. In the end this is what happened but we were accused by the Russians of moving

Nato's border up to theirs, whereas they had dissolved the Warsaw Pact—the military alliance between the USSR and its Eastern European satellites—in 1992. Who was the aggressor? Events since then have put a different gloss on all this, with the annexation of Crimea and invasion of eastern Ukraine. But who can say if things would have been different if the West had acted differently?

As my time in this fascinating job passed, I started to look for another job, one involving promotion and an embassy of my own. This proved extremely difficult and every time I put my name forward for something I fancied, I was turned down. I think the fact that the Office wanted to free my job up for another officer may have been key in the end and I was offered the chance to go to Hungary as ambassador, but only after two years as a member of the Senior Directing Staff at the Royal College of Defence Studies, one of the Ministry of Defence's senior staff colleges. I took this deal, though not without a heavy heart.

Southern Africa

My Southern African experience started by chance. It was 1977. I was working in a backwater and I felt stuck in a rut. My first marriage had broken up and I needed to move on. After some chats with the Personnel people I found myself in a new and exciting position as the desk officer for Namibia, formerly South West Africa, once a German colony, then a UN mandate held by South Africa and now just a territory occupied by South Africa but with its status hotly disputed by the UN and a rebellious black population. There was international pressure to resolve this troublesome problem. Southern Africa faced not only the challenge of apartheid but also civil war in its newly independent neighbours (Mozambique, to its north, facing east towards Madagascar, and Angola, to the north of Namibia on the Atlantic coast to the west), as well as the unresolved issue of Rhodesia where a bitter guerrilla war was being waged to wrest power from the white-minority regime.

I knew little about all this when I began my new role, and so was on a steep learning curve. Britain had joined the US, Canada, France and Germany (still the Federal Republic or West Germany as unification was thirteen years off) in a 'contact group' to broker a settlement between the South Africans and the other parties involved, including the legal Namibian political parties (black and white) and the South West Africa People's Organisation (SWAPO), which was waging a guerrilla war from southern Angola. I was the anchor man for the British side and found myself, for the first time, dealing with the foreign secretary, at that time David Owen, young, dynamic and, I have to say, prickly. At an early meeting with him I was unable to answer a question he threw at me, a factual question to which I should have known the answer. He told me to get out. It was salutary. Later that day we returned with the correct answer and all was well.

The Contact Group worked hard and well. We saw all the people necessary and after quite a short time produced a plan for the independence process, including UN-supervised elections, in the best British tradition, which won favour and was endorsed by the UN Security Council in its Resolution 435. We assumed that the job was now done and that all would move forward to a peaceful settlement of this long-running issue. We were wrong. The South Africans sought reasons for not proceeding and in the end there was deadlock which lasted until 1989, long after I had moved on. Only then was it possible, after much had changed in South Africa, to implement the Contact Group's plan. But it worked, more or less as planned in 1977. I take a little pride in my small role in this.

I returned to Southern African affairs in 1983 when, after an enjoyable secondment to the then Department of Energy, I became deputy Head of the Foreign Office's Southern Africa Department. We oversaw the complex relationship between Britain and apartheid South Africa, where this country still had many important interests and relationships, and of course a history of collaboration and alliance going back to the First and Second World Wars. David Owen and his successor foreign secretaries had done much to strengthen policy towards South Africa, building up a code of conduct for British companies and the way they behaved in the country, and developing our relations with the black and mixed-race communities, with good people appointed to consular and consul general jobs that they would not hitherto have been considered for, and where they could get close to people in the African townships.

My time in this role was dominated by one event. In September 1984 six South African political dissidents entered our consulate in Durban and sought political refuge from the South African authorities. This was a major event in our tricky relations both with the South African government, who wanted us to expel them, and the political opposition in South Africa, and here at home with the very active and vociferous Anti-Apartheid Movement (AAM). In London our job was to advise ministers on the correct political and legal response. Our advice was not to expel the dissidents but let them leave in their own time, but equally not to concede political asylum.

It was a difficult balance. We came under great pressure from the South Africans, who argued that we were in breach of international law, and from the AAM and its parliamentary supporters here at home to do the decent thing and defend the rights of the occupants of our consulate. In practical terms this was difficult. The consulate was small, in an office block with no built-in facilities and no toilets. Portaloos were installed with other domestic facilities, and food and drink provided.

It was all extremely uncomfortable for the British staff and for our embassy and for us in London. We worked endlessly as the crisis unfolded. At one point I held a meeting in the Foreign Office at midnight with a minister and the permanent under-secretary to deal with some urgent issue that had arisen. In the end the six dissidents left of their own accord and it was all over, apart from a not-very-happy post mortem on the hows and whys and did-we-get-it-all-right? No winners there.

As always, I moved on, to happy times in Warsaw. From there I was plucked, at the end of 1988, to move to Zimbabwe as Deputy Head of Mission. I was disappointed. I could see that Poland was on the move and I wanted to be part of that movement, to use my expertise and excellent contacts to follow and influence whatever was going to happen. I had to wait another three years for that to be possible. Instead I was to test my skills and abilities in a quite difficult environment, in a country with an African majority government carrying the legacy of a bitter war against a minority white population, about 100,000 of whom still remained in the country. The whites were mostly of British origin. Britain was also, and unhappily , the former colonial power.

The key thing was to build a network of good contacts among the black majority. These were the people in charge and with whom we had to do business and try to influence. I made an early and avoidable error. Shortly after I arrived in Harare and began work I met a black businessman, a director of the British company Metalbox. I invited him for lunch. It proved fascinating. The man was, it turned out, a key player in the ruling ZANU(PF) party and a member of its politburo, which was organised like a Communist party. Shortly afterwards he rang and invited me to join him at a barbeque at his farm, with other ZANU(PF) senior people. As it happened I was committed on the day in question. I should have cancelled my engagement and jumped at the chance my new contact offered. Instead I declined, thinking that there would be other chances. There weren't. I never saw him again. A lesson in African pride and my own foolishness.

It proved hard for any of us in the British mission to build close relationships with black Zimbabweans. Perhaps there was too much history and perhaps we didn't count as much as we thought we did. Although I worked on diligently I was never able to make up for my blunder. In the end I spent much of my time plotting the unending story of Zimbabwe's economic woes and the efforts of the international community to save

Zimbabwe from itself. I also watched the decline of political life, mired by corruption and nepotism and growing violence. We were reluctant to report this, in spite of all that we heard (often from white Zimbabweans who we felt could not be trusted as a source), mainly because we lacked evidence.

Fortunately, there were two events which brightened my professional time there. The first was my second encounter with Mrs Thatcher, who visited Zimbabwe in early 1989. As usual I arranged this visit and as usual it all went well. There was the habitual tense briefing dinner with her and her husband Denis, who called Zimbabwe 'God's own country' (I was not sure what the fiercely anti-colonialist president Robert Mugabe would have made of that), and then talks with the president, and, best of all, a tripartite visit with Mugabe and President Samora Machel of Mozambique to the British Military Training Team at Nyanga, on the Mozambique border where the British army trained Mozambiquan soldiers to fight the South-African-supported Renamo opposition movement in their own country.

We all flew up there, courtesy of the Zimbabwe air force, with Mrs T insisting on sharing a plane with the two presidents. When we landed at Nyanga there was confusion as the Zimbabwean-provided transport tried to accommodate all the VIPs who had arrived. I had arranged for British mission Land Rovers to be available and hopped into one, only to see Charles Powell, Mrs T's private secretary, looking unsure about what vehicle he would be travelling in. I opened the door of our car and he got in, with some relief. I suspect it was the first time he appreciated my presence. For her part the Prime Minister was, as always, superb. Mugabe and Machel both respected her and enjoyed her company, even if they were poles apart politically.

The second bright moment was the state visit by the Queen.

Meeting the Queen on her arrival at Harare Airport, Zimbabwe in 1991.

Zimbabwe was to host the September 1991 Commonwealth Heads of Government Meeting. The Queen combined her presence at this with a full visit, her first, to Zimbabwe. It fell to me to oversee the planning and management of this. It took six months of my time and involved orchestrating everything to the finest detail. The visit was to take Her Majesty to Bulawayo, in the west of the country, and to Great Zimbabwe, the brick-built ruins of a once-formidable city in the south east, as well as to Harare. Mugabe told us that, if the Queen wished, she could visit the grave of Cecil Rhodes in the Matopos Hills. She didn't but Mugabe's attitude contrasts starkly with that of today's anti-colonialists.

There was also a weekend off, at a safari camp in Hwange National Park. I walked it all, including spending a weekend planning the safari (I slept in the bed later occupied by HM). It was fun but hard work. Although I was present when the

Queen arrived and left, apart from that, I hardly spoke to her, sadly. My moment of glory came however, at the end of the visit when I was summoned to see her and the Duke of Edinburgh, and she made me a Commander of the Royal Victorian Order in acknowledgment of the service I had provided. I was thrilled (and so was my mother). I remember talking with one of the more senior figures in my first department in the Foreign Office in 1969, when he said that all he really wanted was a 'K'. I had to ask him what that was. It was of course a knighthood, a KCMG. I did not get one but I am very happy with my CVO. Happily I was to see more of the monarch later in my career but had no inkling of that at the time.

Interludes

The accounts of my jobs at home and abroad suggest that it was all work and no play. This is far from the truth. I made a point of enjoying myself, and did so in various ways. Zimbabwe was a great country for someone like me. Not only could I play tennis and swim (we had a pool at our house, like many Zimbabweans) and run—I was a keen member of the Harare Athletic Club—but there was the bush, or the *bundhu* as it is called. I had been to a game park once on a visit to South Africa but Zimbabwe had much more to offer.

We not only went regularly to Hwange, where the Queen went, but to lots of other wildlife parks as well. I also went on a five-day canoeing trip on the Zambezi river, in the Mana Pools national park, where I took my best photo ever of a bull elephant charging towards me. It was an exciting moment, and could have been terrifying, but the guide, standing beside me, assured me that I was not in danger as it was a mock charge, not a serious one; the elephant's ears were outstretched, not pinned back, and his head was up not down. I took his word for it and, as he said, kept taking the photos. Phew!

Best of all, I spent nearly a week walking in the Matusadona wilderness area, on the banks of the big, artificial lake Kariba, with two guides, each carrying a rifle, which they spent much time cleaning but never had to fire. We slept on the ground in the open, after walking all day, carrying everything we needed except water, which we collected from the plentiful streams. It was wonderful.

I have been back to central Africa twice since then, both times walking in the bush, just me and one or two guides. I recommend it. You see so much more and appreciate the birds and insect life so much more, as well as the thrill of seeing animals at their level, as opposed to looking at them from a Land Rover. There are risks, and I was always on the look-out for snakes, but they are very seldom seen.

It wasn't hard to enjoy oneself in Poland either. In the 1970s and 1980s when few Poles had cars and traffic was light, it was simple to get out of Warsaw and there were lots of lakes within easy reach, with fresh-water swimming that was fun and safe. In the late 1980s I was able to get away to the weekend cottage I had rented near Różan. This was about 100 kilometres from the capital and it took an hour each way, so we could be there in the light on a Friday evening in summer and stay all weekend. The cottage had electricity and water, which I had to pump up from a tubewell. It also had mice, but they did not bother us. And the position was idyllic, next to the kind of farm you can only dream of nowadays: a young family with no tractor, just a horse and cart and water from a well, with chickens in the yard.

I loved it there. The cottage was set in a meadow, full of wild flowers, on land that had not been cultivated for a long time and that had never seen herbicide or pesticides. On a warm day it was full of butterflies, with many species present. and often I think of it as the place where I first became interested in lepidoptery. Curiously, it was at the cottage itself that I first saw the wonderful Camberwell Beauty, as it emerged from its chrysalis below the door sill of the front door. I saw one again in Hungary, where I pursued my interest at Petneházy, just outside Budapest, which rivalled the Polish cottage for the abundance of species and the health of the countryside. I think two sightings in a lifetime of a Camberwell Beauty is pretty good, though I wouldn't mind a third.

We had had a cottage before, in Canada where I spent two uneventful years (1979–81) as Economic Secretary to the British mission in Ottawa. The job was tedious and I did not have enough to do. It was a shame, as this was a pretty momentous period in international affairs—the US Embassy hostages in Iran and the Soviet intervention in Afghanistan—but Ottawa was a backwater for us at that time.

There was, though, an upside. I loved the outdoor life and for one of the two summers I was there I rented a cottage in the Gatineaux Hills, to the north of Ottawa, in Quebec. The cottage was on a lake and we had a rowing boat, a small sailing dinghy, and a diving raft. It was heaven. I spent every weekend and some longer spells, including one with the children from my first marriage and with my parents. They all loved it. We again encountered mice and bats—but so what? The lake was marvellous and I could not only swim in it but fish. I caught smallmouth bass, which I would cook for dinner. Even the cold winters could be enjoyed with skiing and skating. On Christmas day 1980 we skated on the Governor General's icerink (a diplomatic privilege) in a temperature of -36 Celsius.

Longer interludes in my Foreign Office career were two secondments, one to the then Department of Energy and one to the Royal College of Defence Studies (RCDS). Both taught me a lot. At Energy (1981–83) I wrestled with the nuclear industry and learned about the enrichment of uranium and the reprocessing of spent fuel rods from reactors. I met interesting, intelligent and accomplished people and worked with an industry which Britain had pioneered but has now, sadly, lost. The experience removed any vestige of snobbery, that the Foreign Office was a cut above the rest of the civil service. It isn't. I could have stayed there and made a career at home, leading a more-or-less normal life but I was tempted back to the Foreign Office by a good job offer.

At the RCDS, where I worked for two years in 1996 and 1997, I was exposed to the utter professionalism of our armed forces. I realised that they were extremely good at selecting able people of real quality and producing high-quality leaders. I also spent time on land, at sea and in the air with them. The barmiest thing I ever did happened on one of these outings, to the RAF at RAF Coningsby. Most of the students (a misnomer really, as they were all very senior officers) took the chance to do a spot of flying in a fast jet. I was offered a single engine prop-driven training aircraft. The tutor took me up and asked what I would like to do. I immediately said: aerobatics. He said OK and so we looped the loop, did a barrel roll and went into a stall turn. He gave me the stick so I appeared to be flying the plane. Fortunately he was there to take over just as I was losing control. It was great fun but I don't think I'd do it again.

People also provided relief from the grind and pressure of work overseas and the strain of living in a foreign country, especially one like Poland where one was under surveillance the whole time. There I was lucky enough to become a good friend of Janusz Onyszkiewicz, Solidarity's brave spokesman. I could always talk to him. In 1988 he was, not for the first time, arrested and taken to prison. I used to go and see his wife to make sure she was OK, gossip and see if there was any news. One day I arrived at the block where they lived and saw, in the distance, Janusz walking towards me. He had just been released. I waited for him and we went up to his flat and had a beer and talked through what had happened. A magic moment.

It was in Poland that I met and became close friends with another Solidarity figure, Zofia Kuratowska, a distinguished doctor and a brave and principled woman, who as a child had been a runner for the insurgents during the 1944 Warsaw uprising, distributing the daily Information Bulletin to the fighters. She became godmother to our youngest daughter, Sophie, before going to South Africa as Polish Ambassador. She died there. I wrote an obituary which the *Times* published.

It is no surprise (though it might have been when I was younger) to discover that there were good people everywhere. Another interlude was my two years in Bangladesh, arriving there just a year after the war with Pakistan which had brought the country to independence. It was a very difficult place to live in, with a monsoon climate and terrible poverty. The British mission was poorly staffed and badly led. But I value my time there both for what it taught me about the developing world, and for the Bengali friends I made. I built a circle of young Bengalis, mainly businessmen, and their wives, and had, after an uncertain start, a wonderful time. I even reached the stage where I could look at the poor and disfigured with sympathy; at the beginning I could only look away. It was an education.

The leadership of the mission improved too, with some changes and in particular the arrival of a new deputy head, Ray Whitney, who later went into parliament. Pleasure in Bangladesh chiefly meant playing tennis at the Officers' Club in central Dacca. I was there almost every day, playing at 6 in the morning, because it was cool at that time of day. In the summer there was only one court and one Saturday afternoon the net wire broke. No replacement was available and so we could not play again until one had been brought from Calcutta. I should add that going to Calcutta was regarded as rest and recreation, since there were restaurants and one could buy alcohol (Bangladesh by contrast was dry) and find shops with things for sale.

I kick myself that I was not more curious and inquisitive, I feel I never really got the best out of the places in which I lived, or of the people—many of them extraordinary—with whom I worked. It's the things I didn't do, the questions I didn't ask but should have done, the people I didn't get to know well enough that upsets me. Of course, I had rather busy jobs, a family at home, and generally lots to occupy me. But I wish I had spent more time looking at Islam in Bangladesh, more time on the Holocaust in Poland and Hungary, and so on. There we are. I suppose everyone feels like this. I certainly do.

Music

Music has accompanied me throughout my life, from singing with my mother, to the school choir, to rock and roll, to the joy of opera. I was lucky in that, later, in Budapest, I found many musical friends and was able to host concerts in the Ambassador's residence and later in the flat that I lived in on Nyúl Utca.

This was a longish journey. It was also a frustrating one. When I was five or six my mother sent me for piano lessons. I was not interested at the time and displayed no aptitude, and they quickly stopped. As a teenager I became interested in the guitar and acquired one which I taught myself to play a little, but not with any accomplishment, and that too was abandoned. In Budapest, at the grand age of 54 I had, for the first time, access to a grand piano, the Residence's Blüthner. It was a beautiful instrument and I decided to have another go at learning. I took lessons for several years and was eventually able to play a Bach prelude and a Chopin nocturne. But these were painfully acquired achievements and, not without heartache and regret, I had to admit, finally, that I did not have the talent to play an instrument with any skill. It is a gift I should love to have enjoyed and I admire and partly envy all who are so gifted. They are fortunate indeed.

Nonetheless, the absence of that talent did not deprive me of musical enjoyment. Apart from a lot of singing as a young person, I was always listening to music. My father in particular played the record player continuously (we first had one on our return from Canada in 1957) and was often buying records. He had grown up in the era of the big band and loved Sinatra and Ellington and Glenn Miller. As I was playing with my Meccano set he would be listening to Sinatra while doing something else, so I learned all the songs in what is now called the 'Great American Songbook'. I also started to listen to pop music and to enjoy its rhythms and wild words. I preferred Presley to the Beatles and I never liked the Rolling Stones or Eric Clapton.

We carry the music of our youth into adulthood with us and so our tastes and knowledge tend to be frozen. Mine certainly were, where pop music is concerned. Fortunately I also took a journey into the classical world. Curiously, my mother played the piano well and was knowledgeable about music but did not encourage me to listen to the composers with whom she was familiar. It was my school friend Tim who first introduced me to Sibelius and Mahler, and my sister who let me play her recordings of Beethoven. These were my first steps. Later I branched out and ventured into Schubert and *lieder*. Perhaps most of all I enjoyed the operas of Mozart and then Puccini and Verdi. What more, after all, can one ask for?

One song has particular importance for me. It is Vaughan Williams's 'Linden Lea'. I think I must have sung this at school but its real impact on me came when the wonderful Janet Baker sang it as an encore in Ottawa in 1980. It is the song I always requested when performers came to the Residence in Budapest and asked if I had any requests. Later, when I began to host little concerts in my Budapest flat and, later, in my house in London, I always asked for this to be sung as the finale. It is a haunting song about a free spirit, about the English countryside, and about our folk tradition. I love it.

Church music is often forgotten these days. Yet for people

of my age the Church of England's *Hymns Ancient and Modern* has been a rich and pleasurable source of music. Singing a hymn every day at school assembly for seven years helps to get the repertoire into the blood. Later, as I explored it a little more adventurously, I found real gems like 'Dear Lord and Father of Mankind' for which Hubert Parry wrote the music. And today I can listen happily to Presley, to a good hymn and to *La Bohème* and think they are all beautiful and to be treasured. Music has enriched my life and I am grateful to the teachers at Winterbourne, and to my parents, for starting me off on this road.

Faith and Other Things

My parents were not church-goers. I think they both however accepted the tenets of the Church of England's version of Christianity and regarded that as 'right'. My father was a keen photographer and worked at weekends for a local photography company what took wedding pictures, and he used to tell me that he always felt something special when he was in the church.

As a child the only time I went to church was with the Cubs and Scouts. When we moved to Sussex there were regular church parades. There was also morning assembly every day at school, although on Fridays boys and girls had separate services in case there was something 'sensitive' to be announced, perhaps to do with sex. So I had a good grounding in the C of E without ever taking an active role or opting in, as it were. All this fell away once I left school after which I had nothing to do with the Church for many years.

When I first got married it felt natural and unarguable, though, that it should be a church wedding. Similarly that my boys should be christened. Divorce meant that the second marriage had to be a register-office affair and yet the girls, when they came along, were also all christened, the third rather splendidly in the Savoy Chapel, to which I had access by dint of my being by then a member of the Royal Victorian Order. But still there was no regular church-going, which was hardly surprising as fewer and fewer people bothered to go to church any longer and the Church of England's role in society was fading.

After the break-up of my second marriage, I found however that I needed something more, perhaps some help, perhaps a place to think privately about deeper things, perhaps a place to repent or to hope. I began to go to Sunday services at Budapest's Church of Scotland church. There was a charismatic priest and the services were quite evangelical but no one questioned my presence there or remarked upon it. It just became a regular thing. I found it helpful. When I finally returned to live in London, I sought and found a similar place, and continue to attend, for the same reasons.

I have also become more interested in the Christian faith and read about it. I bought a nineteenth-century Bible and was given *Cruden's Concordance*, the crib that everyone should have. I am passionately attached to the 1662 *Book of Common Prayer* and the King James translation of the Bible. Why? What is it that, at a time of rapidly declining faith in Britain as a whole, I am clinging to? I have tried to explain it to myself and sometimes others. Firstly, I do love the liturgy, the language, the sheer profundity of what I hear and read. Then there is the sense of communion with a group of people who get something similar out of it all. There is peace and tranquillity, if only for a short time. There is atmosphere and emotion. Sometimes there is music, and there is no beating some of our great hymns, both the words and the tunes. Then there is the sense of being part of something very old, going back millennia. You only have to sing a psalm to feel that and to think that those words, sung or recited three or four thousand years ago, are still relevant today.

I would not dream of forcing my own thoughts and beliefs, if that is what they are, on others. This is a place I have come to after a longish journey and which suits me. It may not suit others. I do think, though, that life without the spiritual is bleaker, poorer and lacking something important. So when my grandson was christened I wrote him a letter saying that I hoped that he would in due course come to value that blessing. Indeed the modern C of E service ends with this hope: 'You have received the light of Christ; walk in this light all the days of your life.' This has everything to do with the values of the Christian faith, values which underpin our whole civilisation and run through our history.

Today, sadly, those values are in question as never before. As ambassador in Budapest I received a Christmas card from the then foreign secretary, Jack Straw. The greeting on the inside was, 'Seasons [sic] Greetings'. I was, and still am, shocked. I wrote to the Foreign Secretary's private secretary and asked why such a card had been sent: leaving aside the grammar (no apostrophe, as in 'season's'), which season was it referring to or was it really referring to all four? I did not of course get a response.

Nonetheless I think I had a point. I did not think Christmas was a season but a festival to celebrate the birth of Christ and in effect the beginning of the Christian religion which shaped Western civilisation thereafter. It gave us the moral framework and the values which underpinned—and still underpin—British society. The foreign secretary's card was a symptom of the moral crisis of our modern society. People seem to have become ashamed of our past, our traditions, even our history and our great achievements as a country. They have become afraid to mention them.

I have never denied the failures that also mar our history but no society is without those. The use of the term 'Common Era', instead of the old 'Anno Domini', is part of that process. The erosion seems endless and forceful. The trouble is that there is no new set of values to replace those that are being trashed and discarded. Even the Common Era brigade uses the birth of Christ as the beginning of modern time. I have no fear of standing up for our past and for the things that have done us all so much good. Perhaps we need Arthur Mee and his easy certainties. It might help.

Budapest

When I arrived in Budapest in April 1998 I did not know that this was to be my last job and last posting with the Foreign Office. I probably didn't think very much about it at the time as there were plenty of other things to tackle. I had a large staff, mainly locally engaged Hungarians but also about twenty UK-based British staff. I had several different roles to perform: representative of the British government, political observer and reporter, commercial salesman for UK Limited, guardian of the local and visiting British community, finance officer (I had to sign off the account every month) and personnel manager. I also had to run a small hotel and restaurant, otherwise known as the Ambassador's Residence. Of course I knew almost nobody and needed to know just about everyone who mattered. It was a busy life and I threw myself into it with all the energy I had.

My time in Hungary was dominated by three things: two elections, both involving a change of government; two wars, in Kosovo and Iraq; and the end of my second marriage. I also ended my diplomatic career there, but more of that later.

My arrival was well timed, as there was an election a month later in which the government, in the hands of the Socialist Party, changed to the Young Liberal Democrats (Fidesz) under Viktor Orbán. These fierce anti-Communists seemed a breath of fresh air after the Socialists, many of whom had been in the

Communist regime. I bent my energy to the task of getting to know the key players. I was helped in this by already knowing, from a meeting in London, the woman who was to be Orbán's foreign affairs private secretary. She proved a huge benefit to me throughout the next four years of this first Orbán premiership. Any time I needed to get a message to Orbán, or learn something about his thinking, or arrange a meeting for a visitor, she opened the door for me. Orbán started promisingly but quite quickly lost his shine and showed the underlying intolerance and ultra-nationalism which has tarnished his government since then. As for me, in learning how to be an effective ambassador I got some things right and some wrong.

The first four years passed quickly. In 2002 another election loomed. By then Hungary had joined NATO and begun its painful integration into the major Western institutions. The economy had not done well and there were signs of corruption in the government. A few weeks before the election I was told by 10 Downing Street that Peter Mandelson, now Lord

The Ambassador's Residence in Budapest. Winter 2000.

Mandelson, would be coming to see the opposition Socialist party. He wanted to discuss the election with them. I therefore rang another good contact who was Socialist leader Péter Medgyessy's close adviser, and arranged a dinner for the three of us with Mandelson at my Residence. It proved a frank, entertaining and instructive lesson in how to get elected, with Mandelson doing the teaching. Mandelson himself was a delight to have as a guest—easy, interesting and good fun. Medgyessy went on to win the election and that dinner sealed my place in his esteem. I was able to work closely with him thereafter and deliver everything that London asked for. The most important of these was to persuade Medgyessy to sign a public letter, along with Tony Blair and other European leaders, supporting the political objectives of the Iraq war.

That war was not my first but it certainly took up my time and energy. It was controversial even in Hungary and I found myself in demand on TV, radio and the press to explain the case for war and to defend what the British and Americans

With Prime Minister Peter Medgyessy at the Queen's Birthday Party, 2002.

were doing. My US colleague Nancy Brinker, an associate of the then president George W Bush and his wife, did not like the public profile and kept her head down, so I took the flak. I cannot say I was comfortable doing this but it was my job. We had a thick briefing folder full of arguments to justify the coalition's actions but the case for war rested on evidence that I was never entrusted with and which we now know was bogus. I was glad when it was all over and the media interest waned.

My first war had been the Kosovo war, the final stage in the break-up of the former Yugoslavia and the end of ethnic cleansing. Hungary had just joined NATO when NATO forces began to bomb Serbia, many overflying Hungary to do so. As with Iraq I promoted the legality of the war and defended our objectives in public, often with my US counterpart, at that time a Democrat appointee called Peter Tufo, who was able and confident. We worked well together. Public opinion was sympathetic, though the Hungarian government, which did not take defence very seriously and was of course a novice in NATO, was rather nonplussed by it all.

George Robertson, the UK defence secretary, paid a visit during the war. The Hungarian minister of defence had just been to London and I had sent a warning message to London not to put too much trust in him. When I met Robertson at the airport on arrival, he lost no time in upbraiding me for this, saying that I had missed a trick by not suggesting he and the Hungarian stand together before the press in public and show the unity of the alliance against the Serbs. A difficult start. At the end of a busy day we met with the Hungarian. He almost immediately suggested a pause in the bombing to allow the Serbs to talk to us. Robertson dismissed this. When we got in the car to go to the airport he looked at me and said, 'I know what you are thinking—don't say a thing!' And laughed. I had been right after all.

As a head of post you get lots of visitors—all sorts, from members of the Royal Family to ministers like Robertson, top businessmen (the CEO of Tesco was a regular visitor as Tesco has large interests in Hungary) and VIPs like Lady Solti, widow of the great Hungarian-born conductor Georg Solti, as well as friends and family. I enjoyed most of their visits but not all. One very senior legal figure in the Blair government came. I set off to meet him at the airport as usual. Unfortunately the plane was very early and when I reached the VIP lounge it was empty as the greeting party, which included the Hungarian ambassador to Britain, had gone out to greet him. When I eventually caught up with our visitor, he was plainly furious with me. I apologised but there was no forgiving this apparently serious sin of protocol and manners.

We struggled through the first day of appointments and meals. The next day, after a rather liquid lunch with the Hungarian minister of justice (an attractive woman), our guest staggered to his feet, complimented the minister and Hungary, and then said how grateful he was to the Hungarian ambassador to London for having had the courtesy to greet him at the aircraft steps. I still cannot understand the pomposity and rudeness which led a senior figure of the Blair government to behave like this.

It was a big contrast with most other visitors, for instance Defence Secretary Geoff Hoon, who came in 2003. He was a delight and such a nice man. We sat up talking till 2 am on his last night, playing 50s rock music, about which he was quite an expert. Cherie Blair, Tony's wife, also came, in her role as a European Human Rights law specialist. She was charming, nice and good to have as a house guest.

I enjoyed a visit by William Hague, then leader of the Conservative Party, not least because he was accompanied by one of my heroes, the wonderful Olympian Sebastian Coe, who

Raising the Loyal Toast at the Queen's Birthday Party, 2002.

was his special adviser. We did the rounds which included a call on Hungarian Prime Minister Orbán. Orbán greeted Hague cordially and then turned to Coe and said, with admiration in his voice, 'And you are the great Coe?' I suppose Hague was used to it but it did rather put him in his place.

Another visitor was Prince Charles. He came for a day in 2000—literally a flying visit. I had already met him in 1999 at a dinner in Britain. He was miserable on that occasion and did not seem any happier in Budapest a year later. Funnily enough, I ran into him at a National Trust house in South Wales a few

years later, long after I had retired. He was attending an event there and did a walk-about to say hello to the general visitors. I shook his hand and chatted to him, without reminding him that we had met before. What was striking was that with Camilla by his side, he was happy and relaxed. His earlier misery was after the divorce and then of course Diana's tragic death. It must have been hell for him.

Perhaps the most fun guest was rock guitarist Jet Harris, who came with a replica group of his former band the Shadows. I held a reception for him, having first bought all the

Shadows records I could find. I played their music all evening. At one time I found myself playing the Residence grand piano with the band's keyboard player. At the end Jet signed one of my records with the motif: 'to my mate Nige, yours Jet'. I still have it.

That was a busy weekend in the year 2000. Hungary was celebrating its own millennium, as it was a thousand years since the establishment of the Hungarian kingdom. I had to go the US ambassador's after the Jet Harris do for his reception marking the millennium and then the next day to Sopron in Western Hungary for an EU event, then back to Budapest to attend Jet's concert. I think the band was pleased when I went backstage to talk to them, and perhaps even surprised. Jet had told me that never in his career had a British ambassador invited him to a party.

The next day was the day of the millennium, and very hot too. There was a formal event in the morning, That was followed by fireworks in the evening. The bridges across the Danube were closed, which made it difficult to get to the government reception at the parliament building but we made it in the end. The next day I wrote a report to London, detailing my activities of the preceding 48 hours. I wondered if UK taxpayers would think this was time well spent and concluded that they might appreciate my party for Jet Harris but not much else.

It was from Budapest that I once again found myself in contact with the Queen. In 1999 the Hungarian president, Árpád Göncz, was invited to Britain on a state visit. I was to accompany him, with my then wife, throughout his visit. It was a very splendid affair. We stayed at Windsor Castle. There was a huge state dinner in Göncz's honour, a visit to Scotland and much else. All very grand. I never got to talk to the monarch, of course—I was much too junior—but it was very special. I later accompanied Göncz's successor, Ferenc Mádl, to London on a working visit. This involved lunch at Buckingham Palace, just eight of us, I think. After the lunch, as we were leaving, the Queen said to me, 'Mr Thorpe, where did we go wrong in Zimbabwe?' What a question! She had of course read her brief and realised that I had been in Zimbabwe when she paid her state visit in 1991. My answer, that we had misread Mugabe, was not a good one. I have often thought about it and I should have said that we failed to appreciate the injustice and anger at the way land had been distributed to white settlers in the former Rhodesia. Land was the crux of the problem. If I ever see her again I would like to explain this.

The Queen is a feature of the life of all ambassadors. Her birthday is our national day abroad and embassies and high commissions (in Commonwealth countries) celebrate the event with a large drinks party, called the Queen's Birthday Party (QBP for short). The guest of honour is of course missing but the party is a splendid one and we always tried to make it the high point of our entertaining year.

In 2002, when the Queen celebrated her Golden Jubilee, I used the QBP to celebrate not just her birthday but the jubilee as well. In doing so I was, I recall, going somewhat against instructions, which were to play the occasion quietly. Instead I arranged a big bash, with two-thousand guests. Both the president and prime minister of Hungary came, which was not typical. The president looked around the garden at the assembled guests and said to me 'The cream of Budapest society is here.' And so it was.

Early on in my time in Budapest, in 1999, my second marriage, which by then had lasted more then twenty years, broke up. It was a very unhappy event and caused untold disruption and wretchedness. It of course entailed a reordering of the way everything to do with our family was managed. It also meant that I had to spend most of my Budapest posting living on my own. This had many downsides. I found that living in a palace was not really to my taste and that I was, of course, lonely. When Cherie Blair thanked me for looking after her, she said 'and don't stay alone in that ghastly house'. Good advice but I was set to do so. Fortunately, for some of the time, I had visits from my daughters, and my eldest daughter Jessie came for every holiday. I was always grateful for this and still am.

All this meant that I was on my own when the attack on the World Trade Centre took place on 11 September 2001. Like many people I remember exactly what I was doing when I heard the news. I was in my office in the splendid British Embassy in downtown Pest when the head of the Embassy Commercial Section rang me to say that the Twin Towers were on fire. 'Come up to Information Section and watch the TV,' she said. I ran up the stairs to the third floor, where the only television in the Embassy was to be found. Staff were gathered round, mesmerised by the inferno that had been, hours earlier, the World Trade Centre. It was too awful to behold, gawping at scenes that now, out of good taste and consideration for the families of those who died, can no longer be shown on television.

When I went home later, I continued to watch the TV. I had forgotten, in the course of events, that my Hungarian teacher was due to come and give me a lesson that evening. She duly arrived, rather nervously, and we watched the unfolding disaster together, she teaching me appallingly necessary words like 'collapse' and 'suicide' as we watched poor people hurl themselves from the windows above the impact points, and then the towers collapsing as the metal structures melted in the heat. I wanted to call my American colleagues but knew I couldn't.

The next morning I gathered my team in the Embassy to consider the implications for us and our work and security.

There were some general instructions from London but on practical issues we took our own decisions. The first was to protect the Embassy from a car bomb attack. We contacted the city council and with its agreement swiftly surrounded our very exposed building with a barricade of large concrete blocks. An armed guard, provided by the Hungarian government, appeared. New procedures for screening visitors to the building were introduced. I started to vary my route to and from the office. Armed guards appeared at the Residence in the Second District as well. Little did we appreciate that these things were for ever, not just for a few months.

There were moments of light relief. For instance, my American colleague, Nancy Brinker was single, like me. This led the Foreign Minister, János Martonyi, to suggest jokingly that the Hungarian government could save money on security if we moved in together. But the reality was that terrorism was changing all our lives, especially those much closer to the scene like Nancy's predecessor, Peter Tufo, with whom I was in touch. A New York lawyer, he told me he was attending funerals of friends, but without bodies.

I mentioned above that the Hungarian government provided an armed guard at the Residence in the Second District after 9/11. After a while, I think in 2003, they decided to withdraw this and so London authorised me to to contract a private security company. A team duly arrived and the first thing they did was to search the perimeter and the the Residence gardens. They opened a large garden shed which for some reason was not in use and discovered two men in it: vagrants, homeless, whatever. Not terrorists. But goodness knows how long they had been there.

By the end of 2002 I was more than conscious that my time in Budapest was nearing its end. I had already been there longer than normal but, under the Foreign Office's new system of applying for jobs, I had not been successful in getting another post. Then the post of Ambassador to Warsaw came up. I applied, thinking I would be a strong, perhaps unbeatable candidate since I had served there twice, spoke very good Polish, knew a lot of people and had a unique background in the region. The Foreign Office thought otherwise. I was disappointed but accepted my fate initially, at least.

By this time the Iraq war had been fought and sort of won, but Iraq was descending into violent chaos. Later, at the end of that year, after I had left Budapest, my friend and dear colleague Roger Short, who was Consul General in Istanbul, was murdered in a car bomb attack on his office. Al Qaeda again. It wasn't over, not by a long chalk. My daughter Jessie and I had visited Roger and his wife in Istanbul. It was very close to the bone.

My disillusion with my employer and my concern about my future now combined and I therefore decided to leave and ask for the early retirement package. There was no message urging me not to do this so my fate was sealed. In June that year I retired from a career of thirty-four years. I have never regretted that, nor looked back. Nor did I look for another job which would use my Foreign Office knowledge and skills. It was time for a change.

Dido

Just before the break-up of my second marriage we acquired a yellow Labrador puppy. We didn't know what to call her but one evening we gave a party at which two of our Hungarian guests performed Dido's lament from Purcell's *Dido and Aeneas*. This was their party piece and is an aria I have never really gone for: it is so mournful. Anyway, our new puppy thought so too and let out a long howl during the performance. Afterwards I said we should call her Dido (a pun on Fido, of course). So Dido she became. What I never expected was that Dido would become my closest companion and friend. After the marriage went wrong and I found myself on my own again, I kept the puppy. She was good for me. I talked to her, walked her and explored Budapest's surrounding woodlands with her. Dido grew up and was really quite well behaved. She took part in all the Residence parties, wandering between the tables at dinners and making friends with all my many guests.

Sadly, Dido passed away shortly after I left the Foreign Office but she lives on, I hope, in the FCO archives. This happened because one day in, I think, 2002 I received a circular message from the person then known as the chief clerk, that is, the head of the Foreign Office's management. He addressed the vexed question of running the palatial establishment which we all lived in as heads of mission, namely the Residence. This was a real burden and one of those many things which the

Dido and me.

Office expected you to take in your stride, with no training or preparation. Anyway, the Chief Clerk was offering a small sum of money to enable us all to appoint a Residence housekeeper. I thought this was a thinly disguised way of letting heads of post, who were mostly male, appoint their wives to this role and so pay them for doing something they had been doing unpaid before. It led me to think about my own position—not unique—of being alone or single. And so I wrote back:

I have been pondering your Circular 425 of 11 June on the appointment of Residence Housekeepers/Managers.

There is no doubt that running a Residence is a burden which deserves sharing and remuneration. As you know, living in a small hotel and restaurant is a 24-hour preoccupation and one is never entirely free of the challenges it brings. It is attractive to share these with somebody else, be it your spouse or somebody else's. It is nice too if the main burden can be handed to somebody who is paid to carry it, which heads of mission certainly aren't.

But I think the biggest burden of all falls on those of us who are single heads of mission. We have no spouse at home to share the work of running the Residence. I for one have been reluctant to take on somebody else's spouse to share this task with, not least because it involves meddling in what passes as home. What to do? Of course, a live-in partner would be good, but luck—so far—is not running my way.

After much consideration I have however produced the ideal solution, at any rate for my situation. It has the strong support of my management officer. I am therefore writing to ask your permission, and that of the PUS (permanent under-secretary) to appoint my dog as Residence Housekeeper/Manager. Her name, by the way, is Dido, a suitably regal name for the incumbent of such an important position.

She has all the requisite qualities. First of all, she is female (and I assume from your telegram that only females may apply for this task). She knows the house intimately: every nook and cranny has felt her presence. She is enormously popular as well as feared by the staff—they love her but are terrified of her bark. Guests, be they ministers or mannequins, are at her beck and call. She is modest in her personal requirements, eating only two meals a day and drinking nothing but water, so sobriety at least can be relied on in the execution of her functions.

No clothing allowance is required as she comes complete with her own fur coat. She has, perhaps above all, undoubted honesty (except for the furtive consumption of the odd left-over) and an extremely equitable temperament, always happy to see me, or for that matter, you.

> And finally, she would win any open and above-board contest for the job, so clear to all are her merits.
>
> I think she would be happy to spend the £300 or so which the job pays. I already share most of my troubles with her. Why not this one too? I look forward to your positive response.

Well, it was a joke of course. To his credit the Chief Clerk replied in similar vein. Dido ruled supreme in my household, in spite of not getting this job. She was much missed after her too-early death.

Hungary and the War

Living for all those years in Poland and Hungary, I reflected a lot on what the Second World War had done to them. Each had had a terrible time. Poland was brutally ruled by the Nazis. The landlord of the house I lived in when I first arrived in Warsaw in 1970 often talked about the war, in which he had grown up. He said that a boy grew up very quickly in those times, seeing so much that was so awful.

For the Hungarians, an ally of Germany, there was the hope of recovery of the lands lost through the Treaty of Trianon at the end of the First World War. This hope was never really realised, even at the zenith of Nazi power. And Hungarian dreams were shattered by the stunning defeat of the Hungarian second army on the Eastern Front in 1943 and then the invasion and conquest of Hungary by the advancing Red Army. The Soviet soldiers were unrestrained in their savagery, the rape of women and the theft of personal possessions. A good friend of mine, a minister in the first Orbán government, told me that in 1945, as a boy, he was in the family home with his parents and siblings sheltering in the basement from the fighting. The door was pushed open and a Soviet soldier came in, gun at the ready. He saw the boy's father and motioned to him to come outside, probably to join the lines of Hungarian men being rounded up to go to labour camps in the Soviet Union. At that moment an officer came in and saw the family. He ordered the soldier to leave the family and the father alone. Such were the chances of life or death at that time.

Of course, there were great differences in their experiences. Poland had fought Nazi Germany and had shown great courage and belief in its opposition. It had also suffered appallingly. But its courage was not uniform and there were sad instances of collaboration and, perhaps most depressing, of betrayal of Polish Jews, in the country that was the centre of the Holocaust. The culmination of that was the pogrom in Kielce in 1946, after the war, following stories that those few Jews who had survived there were drinking the blood of a Polish child. Anti-Semitism was, it seems, a great survivor and resulted in 1968 in many of the remaining Jewish population being driven out of Poland under a Communist government imposed on Poland by the Soviet Union. Sadly today, Poland is rewriting its history to make clear that no Pole played a role in the Holocaust.

This is a terrible failure by Poles to come to terms with their country's history. It contrasts starkly with Germany, where Germans have made heroic efforts to confront their past.

Hungary, I am afraid, falls into the same trap as the present Polish government and its supporters. It had a bad twentieth century, being on the losing side in two world wars before being occupied by the Soviets and having to live with a Communist government. There are numerous examples from the Communist period of Hungarians killing Hungarians, but at least there was the courage of the 1956 uprising which, to some extent, mitigates what happened. That stands out against the reluctance, which I encountered so often, to face up to the bad choice made in 1940 to join the Axis powers, compounded by the decision in 1941 to take part in the German attack on the USSR. Hungarians say they had no choice, though historically this is not correct. There were sensible and brave people who argued for a different course, albeit in very difficult circumstances.

I always argued that the Czechs and Poles faced the same challenge and took a different line, though with no better result. Count Pál Teleki, who was prime minister in the Horthy government of 1941, chose to shoot himself rather than face the consequences of the decision (in which he had, with qualifications, acquiesced) to allow German forces to pass through Hungary to invade Yugoslavia. To him that decision was too shameful to live with. And of course, the Hungarians were complicit in the deportation of many of the country's Jewish population, of whom about 500,000 were murdered. The vehement anti-Semitism of the Hungarian Arrow Cross government went on to the bitter end, as the tragic monument to those shot in January 1945 on the banks of the Danube in Budapest, near the Chain Bridge, shows.

And now the Orbán government is also rewriting history to justify the events of the past and make the Hungarians look as though they fought steadily for their country's independence. It was not like that, and this type of myth-making flies in the face of objective, honest analyses that seek to understand events and where necessary confront them.

Retirement

I always date my retirement from 2007, when I stopped working. In fact I retired from the Foreign Office in 2003, very fed up and disillusioned with a Diplomatic Service that I felt uncomfortable with. Failure to get Warsaw was part of it; it was a big disappointment, though with hindsight life there would have been just like Budapest on a slightly bigger scale. So perhaps I didn't miss much. And I was fed up with the Office's obsession with management rather than effective Embassies (though I accept that only a well-managed embassy can be effective—we were). In the end I asked for and was granted early retirement, with a rather generous package. However, I was pretty sure that I needed to go on working and earning, so I began to look for a job. Through contacts I had made in Budapest I was finally offered a chance with the telecoms giant Vodafone. This included the rather unusual situation of going on working in Budapest for a while. I did this and although it was a bit awkward at times, in the end it worked out well. And Vodafone in any case duly transported me to the Group Headquarters in Newbury to run the charitable foundation they had established. Although I only spent four years with the company this opportunity was really the key to my retirement. I learnt about the charitable sector in Britain, how charities run, how grants are made and so on. When I finally left the company, I decided that this was what I wanted to do. I also had been able to rebuild my shattered finances, which was not unimportant.

Settling in London again, after nearly 10 years away, was not quite straightforward. Work so defines who you are that when you are not working, you have no job to identify you and your place in the scheme of things. This can be a challenge, as all of us have to face this in some form and accept that perhaps the most meaningful part of our lives is over. I have to say that I did not spend much time grieving over this. It is after all amazing how many things there are to do, if you look for them. I followed up the Vodafone charitable link and although I did not get the CEO position in a charity that I thought I wanted, I still found third sector organisations that were interested in what I had to offer. So, I have spent a busy and fulfilling retirement, working with a number of charities, and I have I hope played a positive role in at least one of them. There is another aspect to this though, not just about the work. For the first time I was playing a part in the wider community, something I had never been able to do before. Apart from charitable work I was also secretary of my tennis club for four years, a job I really loved and where I think I made a contribution to the reform of the Club's structure and operation. (Tennis has been a key activity and I still play four or five times a week). I can boast of setting up two residents' associations, and being active as a private person in a range of local issues, something impossible when I was working. Also at a private level, I could pursue my love of gardening. I was fortunate to find an allotment, well, two in fact, by dint of joining waiting lists, though I found two one too many, so gave up the one that was furthest away. Add to that continuing to make things (I never buy something if I can make it), reading, music and the cinema and there is plenty to be happy about. I have also lived in one place for 13 years, after a life of regular moves both at home and abroad—I count 17 moves in all, probably above the average for a resident of Britain. This has its own satisfactions and compensates for some of the frustrations of living in other people's houses, and countries, for so long.

This has also been a period of once again having a family life. Being in London has meant I can see my daughters and the elder son from my first marriage, and now my grandson. That has been a great pleasure. I am very proud of my children and feel blessed to have them.

I also became a part-time, unqualified teacher. I discovered that school children today study as history the period through which I worked, and that they welcomed the chance to hear from someone who had been there and done it, as it were. So I have lectured to classes studying the history of the Soviet Union and the Cold War. I present myself as living history - well, it is true. I also undertook something that I regard as the most satisfying thing I have ever done, which was to tutor two young women who were struggling in their sixth form courses, and help them to get back on track and to make it all the way to university. When I look back on my busy retirement this is the thing I think I did best, and found most worthwhile. Not bad, I would say.

My engagement with public affairs didn't quite end with retirement. I have been a convinced European since before Britain joined the European Economic Community and I was appalled when David Cameron announced the referendum on EU membership. I campaigned vigorously for the Remain camp, but knew, from talking to members of the public in the week of the vote, that it was not going to work out well. Afterwards, like so many, I supported the demand for a second referendum, went on marches and donated money. I even became a team member of the campaign and organised a letter to the media, signed by 43 former British ambassadors, demanding another referendum. It was all to no avail and after the result of the 2019 election I finally, reluctantly, accepted that we would inevitably leave the EU. In doing so I accepted the 2016 result as well. I am resigned to the consequences, knowing at last that I have no ability to influence what happens. It is an odd feeling, for at one time I could have a say in what went on, albeit perhaps a marginal one.

Finale

This is only a fraction of an autobiography but it records the essence of my childhood and describes significant episodes from my adult life. It also includes some reflections on things that have affected me. It is probably a little arrogant of me to believe that my story and indeed my reflections are of interest to any but, at most, my family and friends. I confess to that arrogance because I think it is remarkable that a boy of my background, whose parents did not go to university and who really had no advantages in life, could have had the life I have had—and so I thought it worth recording.

Looking back, I always think I belong to a very fortunate generation, perhaps the most fortunate ever. I am always moved by the Church of England prayer, 'Give us peace in our time, O Lord'. How meaningful that is. I never experienced war, with all its hardships, dangers and loss. I had a free and very good education and I did not leave university burdened with debt. I have benefited from the National Health Service and antibiotics, and have enjoyed on the whole good health.

I entered the workforce at a time of full employment. Getting a job was not hard. I was never unemployed and never faced uncertainty about my position. When it came to buying a house, prices were always reasonable and within my reach.

It was chance that brought me to the Foreign Office and gave me the career I had. I still do not know why I was accepted. Perhaps it was because the 1960s were a time of extraordinary social mobility. I moved upwards, I suppose you would say. I think it remarkable and am grateful to such people as R.A. Butler of the 1944 Education Act and Clement Atlee and Harold Macmillan, who presided over my childhood and set the framework for much of what happened to me.

I was fortunate too to grow up in a free country with an established democracy and robust, well-run institutions. Corruption is not something we have to worry about. I have always felt I could trust the police and the judicial system. Our constitution allows the individual and not a political ideology to predominate. Perhaps one has to live in countries where things are different to appreciate how fortunate Britons are. We have never faced the appalling dilemmas experienced, for instance, by the citizens of Communist Poland, where you had to join the party, even if you didn't believe in any of its ideology, to gain an easier life. In contrast, to decline to join or, for the brave, to go into opposition carried penalties, not just for the person concerned but for his or her family and friends. Our democracy and all that goes with it are treasures that we should preserve at all costs.

Notwithstanding this, the Britain I represented overseas changed almost beyond recognition during the course of my career. Immigration is part of that change—perhaps the most visible part—but is not the whole story. There are profound differences in social attitudes, the class system has eroded, society has opened up, prosperity has increased, new issues to do with identity and sexuality have emerged, and so on. Each time I returned to Britain to live and work, I returned to a country that had changed quite radically. Abroad, one was not conscious of this and I think we were always, inevitably, behind the curve.

Physically the country changed too. Towns and cities grew,

the old villages I had known as a child in Sussex became homes for commuters, and the character of the population was transformed as agricultural work dried up and the very local nature of life ebbed away. It can all be quite hard to cope with and one needs to gulp sometimes, to count to ten and say, yes, that is all right, even if things one treasures are endangered by the deep social and economic transfigurations.

I am not sure, if I am honest, that all that has happened is for the best. The Britain I knew as a child has gone for ever—indeed one could say that the Britain that people fought for and died to defend has gone for ever. But then many of those who fought voted for fundamental change in 1945. That was the start of many of the things that I have benefited from. And all the changes have taken place in, and been permitted to happen because of, an unprecedented and very long period of peace and prosperity.

My wish now is that my children and their children will have the same good fortune as I have had. I so wish it.

Printed in Great Britain
by Amazon

59805537R00066